INSURANCE AS A SECOND LANGUAGE

To Kim

Insurance Rocks!

INSURANCE AS A SECOND LANGUAGE

A COMIC GUIDE TO EVERYTHING
YOU NEED TO KNOW ABOUT INSURANCE

DALE IRVIN

INSURANCE AS A SECOND LANGUAGE

A Comic Guide To Everything
You Need To Know About Insurance

Kleenan Press
P.O. Box 9061
Downers Grove, Illinois 60515

Phone: (630) 852-7695
E-Mail: info@DaleIrvin.com
Web Site: www.daleirvin.com

ISBN: 0-9657420-2-4

Cover Design & Typesetting: Ad Graphics, Inc.

Printed in the United States of America

First Edition

1 2 3 4 5 6 7 8 9 10

Dedication

This book is dedicated to everyone
who purchased policies from me during
my career in life insurance sales.
Thank you both.

Table of Contents

Foreword or Read This Part First

One of the most confusing topics to the average person is the topic of insurance. Since we tend to fear that which we don't understand, a majority of us normal people are scared to death of insurance, and in my policy, being scared to death pays double indemnity.

Since we fear insurance, we naturally tend to fear anyone who tries to sell us insurance. This person, who is usually a close relative, is only trying to help us, but because we don't speak the same language we don't know what we need or what to ask. It is for that reason that I wrote this book. It is about time that somebody bridged the gap between what we think we know and what we would like to know.

My qualifications to write this manuscript are two-fold. First, I have a professional background in insurance. After graduating from college, I was recruited by a major life insurance company to help them distribute their product. I was a life insurance professional for six and one half months before I completely ran out of relatives. That insurance company is currently out of business although I don't think it was completely my fault.

Realizing that insurance sales were not my forte, I turned to comedy. This book contains everything I learned from combining these two vocations. Please remember that this book is designed for entertainment purposes and nothing herein should be construed as the truth. For actual information about insurance, please contact your professional insurance agent. One of them probably lives next door to you.

"If You Break Your Leg, Don't Come Running to Me."

The concept of risk assessment

"If You Break Your Leg, Don't Come Running to Me."

The concept of risk assessment

Insurance has never been the problem. Risk has been the problem and insurance has been a way of dealing with it. But we have never been afraid of the Risk Man, indeed, I don't think I've ever even met Risk Man but he sounds like a superhero. Insurance Man, on the other hand, scares the bejammers out of us.

When I use the term "Insurance Man" I am using it in the general sense because it is easier than saying "Insurance man and/or woman, including women who used to be men and men who used to be women."

The reason we fear Insurance Persons, is because we fear risk. What we need to do is to get a deeper understanding of what risk is all about so we can lose our fear of it. Then, once we have rid ourselves of risk phobia, we can concentrate on the other reasons the Insurance Person scares us.

Risk was invented in 10,000 BC when Trog told his friend Ug to pet the dinosaur. Ug knew there was a risk involved but since Trog was bigger than he was and was holding the town's only club, he weighed the risk of petting the dinosaur as the lesser. A few months later, Ug officially changed his name to Lefty and had a heightened awareness of risk.

The seeds of risk were planted even earlier than that when Adam weighed the odds of eating fruit against feeling the wrath of God. Ever since that time, men have made a lot more bad decisions than we have good ones.

The earliest form of insurance began in China during the Wang Chung Dynasty. It was right about this time that the Chinese invented gunpowder and used it to manufacture fireworks. Unfortunately, fireworks soon led to people losing fingers and hands because they failed to follow the simple directions of "light fuse and get away." The loss of appendages then led to the creation of insurance. One could say that this first use of insurance was a "hands on" event but then one would be guilty of a terrible pun.

The first Chinese insurance company was known as Lloyds of Nanking. It should not be confused with the well-known Lloyds of London because over in China that company was known as Roids of Rondon.

Insurance first appeared in 14th century Europe when Medieval Life Insurance opened its doors in 1346. Business was brisk and policy sales flourished. In 1347 the Bubonic Plague arrived and Medieval Life Insurance went out of business.

It was 1490 before serious attempts were once again made to sell life insurance. About this time, a young adventurer named Christopher Columbus was weighing the risk of discovering a new route to India against falling off the edge of the earth. After careful thought and deliberation, Columbus said, "What the heck." And started planning his journey.

One day, a young man named Ernie visited Columbus at his office and asked him if he would like to insure his voyage. He told him that he could provide marine insurance, personal liability insurance, mutiny insurance, and hostile attack insurance with double indemnity if you are eaten by a cannibal. Columbus bought the whole package and then asked Ernie why he hadn't recommended any life insurance. Ernie replied, "I looked up explorer on the mortality tables and you would be rated at least triple."

Obviously Ernie thought that insuring Columbus' life was a risky business, which is a perfect example of how risk and insurance go hand in hand.

"Risky Business" is the name of the delightful 1983 comedy starring a young Tom Cruise and a sexy Rebecca DeMornay. In the movie, Cruise's character Joel Goodson, has to weigh the risk of spending the night on an el train with a good looking hooker or getting in trouble with his parents. Of course, Joel went with the hooker. This was taking a risk. What happened next, however, could have been avoided by insurance.

If you remember the movie, Joel dumps his dad's Porsche into the lake and has his house robbed of all belongings by an irate pimp. He didn't know how to explain this to his parents. If he had had adequate insurance, this would not have been a problem.

Insurance would have covered getting his dad a new car and getting his mom all new furniture. They would have been happy, Joel would have still spent time with the hooker, and the pimp would have gotten a whole truckload of good stuff. It would have been a win-win-win situation. If only they had enough insurance.

Risk has been around for a long time and as long as we have politicians running this country it will be around for a long time to come. The best way to keep up with risk is to follow the 10 simple rules of risk management.

Ten Simple Rules of Risk Management

1. Never draw to an inside straight.
2. In a bar fight, always help the bigger guy.
3. Don't buy anything you see advertised on late night TV if you have been drinking tequila all day and have access to your credit cards.
4. When in doubt, spit it out.
5. Never take anyone up on the offer to pull their finger.
6. Most arguments can be ended with the 5 magic words, "You're right dear. I'm sorry."
7. Avoid betting on the Cubs to win the World Series.
8. When asked the question, "Does this outfit make me look fat?" get out of your chair and slowly back out of the room without uttering a word.
9. Do not pet a dog if he feels sticky.
10. To avoid ever forgetting your wife's birthday or anniversary, play the same numbers in the Lottery every day.

Since we all face risks every day, it helps if we know the odds of any particular risk occurring at any particular time. For instance, we all take the risk of being hit by a cow falling from a ten-story building every time we walk by a ten story building in Wisconsin. This is the reason there are so few tall buildings in Wisconsin. They have measured the risk of getting hit by a cow diving from a tall building and decided to do something about it.

Of course, had they examined the true risk ahead of time they would have realized that the odds of this happening at any given time are approximately 500 bazillion to one. This is due to a little known fact that cows are not only afraid of heights, but they can't climb stairs and don't fit into elevators so it is almost impossible for them to get to the top of a tall building. In this case, the odds of the event occurring are classified as slim-to-none and the risk is very low.

Since risk is all around us, we need to more fully understand the ramifications of risk. For instance, if you are debating whether or not to purchase lightning insurance, you should know that your chances of being hit by lightning are 60,000 to one. However, if you live in a cave and never venture outside, those odds drop dramatically, to about a billion to one. Likewise, your odds of being eaten by a wild boar are about 200,000 to one but if you don't invite any wild boars into your home your odds improve to 250,000 to one.

Rather than "boar" you with further statistics, refer to the following examples for your odds on just about anything.

What Are The Odds?

Sitting on the toilet before realizing that you are out of paper? Having to run down to the store with your pants around your knees to get more.	**1 out of 10.** **1 out of 100.**
Running to answer the phone and then finding out it is a telemarketer. Running to answer the phone and then realizing that it was the phone on the TV show you are watching that was ringing.	**1 out of 3.** **1 out of 5.**
Parking in the handicapped spot at the supermarket and not getting caught. Going to the supermarket and coming home with everything except the item you originally went for.	**1 out of 2.** **EVEN.**
Driving more than three blocks without fastening your seatbelt. Driving more than three blocks with your turn signal on.	**1 out of 5.** **1 out of 2 but it's not because I'm getting older. I just don't realize the darn thing is still going.**

Having people mistake you for a famous celebrity.	**1 out of 1,000.**
Having people mistake you for somebody they saw on America's Most Wanted.	**EVEN.**
Mistaking the tube of Preparation H for toothpaste.	**You only have to do this once and I guarantee it will never happen again.**
Mistaking Viagra for sleeping pills.	**Boy, you talk about being up all night…**
Finding one more beer in the back of the refrigerator.	**1 out of 100.**
Finding food in the refrigerator that you bought when Carter was president.	**1 out of 5.**
Forgetting to zip up.	**Odds are very high if you are seven years old or younger.**
Even worse, forgetting to unzip.	**Odds are very high if you are 85 or older.**

Winning the lottery. Telling people that you are going to continue working even though you just won $100 million. (I don't know why people do this but my guess is so they can lord it over their boss by driving a Rolls Royce to work and parking it right next to his two-bit Lexus.)	**1 in a million.** **1 out of 2.**
Ever dating a super model. Ever dating a regular model. Ever dating a model figure of a real person.	**1 in two million.** **1 in one and a half million.** **1 out of 10 if you're lucky.**
Putting an eye out. Putting an eye out while running with scissors.	**1 out of 2,347.** **1 out of 1. Just ask any mom.**
Winning the Publisher's Clearing House Sweepstakes. Buying a magazine subscription thinking that is going to improve your chances.	**1 out of infinity.** **1 out of 5 because you are very gullible.**

Having a bird poop on your head. Having an elk poop on your head.	**1 out of 20.** **The odds of this ever happening are astronomical but if it does, you are having a very bad day.**
Being able to open a bag of airplane peanuts without having to use scissors. Getting a pair of scissors through airport security.	**1 out of 30.** **Yeah right. Send me a letter from jail.**
Getting electrocuted while turning on the TV set to watch The Food Network. Choking to death while eating a TV dinner.	**3 out of 5.** **6 out of 10.**
Being injured by a flying BINGO marker in the church basement. Being injured by the little old lady sitting next to you for yelling out "BINGO" before she does.	**1 out of 10,000.** **EVEN.**

Drawing to a royal flush while playing strip poker.	**1 in a million.**
Ever getting to play strip poker with people you really would want to see naked.	**1 in 2 million.**
Being up the creek without a paddle.	**A regular day at the office.**
Being up the creek without a boat.	**An exceptionally lousy day at the office.**
Ever finding a Playboy magazine in your doctor's waiting room.	**INFINITE.**
Finding any magazine printed in this millennium in your doctor's waiting room.	**INFINITE PLUS ONE.**
Finding hard candy and caramels available in your dentist's waiting room.	**IT'S CALLED ESTABLISHING FUTURE BUSINESS.**

Having a heart attack.	**1 out of 25.**
Having a heart attack in the doctor's office or while visiting in a hospital.	**YOU'VE GOT TO BE KIDDING.**
Having a heart attack while on the 18th hole of the golf course when you are playing the game of your life and all you have to do to win $1000 is to sink a two-foot putt.	**EVEN.**
Having absolutely nothing go your way.	**EVEN.**
Having everything go your way.	**IMPOSSIBLE.**
Calling your significant other by the wrong name during a moment of intense intimacy.	**This is another one of those things that you will only do once, and you'll never forget it.**
Ever being able to recover from that.	**1 out of 10 bazillion.**

Looking your age if you just turned 21.	**5 to 1 against. Nobody looks their age at 21, that's why the liquor stores have to card them.**
Looking your age if you just turned 81.	**Take this bet if you can get it. You will look your age, your wife's age, and your dog's age if you even make it this far.**

In the end, everyone must decide the degree of risk with which they are comfortable, then, buy insurance to fill your needs. You should also buy insurance whenever the dealer has an ace showing.

Now that you know everything there is to know about risk, it's time to take an in depth look at the different varieties of insurance available.

You Bet Your Life...
Insurance

"Say the secret word and an agent will be at your door in 2 minutes."

2

You Bet Your Life...Insurance

"Say the secret word and an agent will be at your door in 2 minutes."

The most common yet least understood form of insurance is life insurance. When you buy life insurance, you are betting that you are going to die before you want to die while the insurance company is betting that you will live a long time and then die a few days after you make your last premium payment.

Life insurance brings with it, its own language and the questions pursuant to that language. Before you engage in a conversation with a life insurance professional, read this chapter and commit it to memory.

Who should own life insurance? Anybody who currently has a life should own some life insurance. After all, you wouldn't buy auto insurance if you didn't drive a car so you shouldn't buy life insurance if you don't have a life. To test if in fact, you do have a life, take this simple quiz.

- ❑ Do you currently watch the Jerry Springer Show five or more days a week?
- ❑ Do you know the names of three or more contestants on Survivor or know the entire cast of a daytime soap opera?
- ❑ Did you ever vote for Ross Perot?

If you answered "YES" to three or more of these questions, you do not need life insurance because you do not have a life.

If you find this quiz to be difficult, just remember this simple poem:

You only need car insurance
If you're going to drive.
You only need life insurance
If you are alive.

I will now entertain questions from the audience.

My life insurance policy mentions my death, which scares the heck out of me. Aren't there any other terms they could use instead of death?

You can request that your insurance company change the term "death" to any of the following:

Kick the bucket, catch a cab, buy the farm, croak, cash in your chips, bite the dust, meet your maker, pushing up daisies, go into real estate, take a dirt nap, call it a day, crap out, check out, curl up one's toes, answer the last roll call, feed the worms, go belly up, hand in your dinner pail, keel over, take the big jump, drop off the twig, throw in your cards, or assume room temperature.

Who should be my beneficiary?

This is a good question and a very important decision for you to make. Choosing your beneficiary is every bit as important as choosing your next tattoo or deciding whether to go with cable TV or a satellite dish. In other words, it is a **really** important decision.

Fortunately, the insurance companies know how tough this choice can be so they allow you to choose more than one beneficiary. First, you select a **primary beneficiary** who is the person you would most like to receive the money from your insurance policy. Next, you pick a **contingent beneficiary** whose job is to watch the primary beneficiary like a hawk, and if they start spending the money on stupid stuff like an indoor ice rink or an air hockey table, they can start a lawsuit to make sure that the money gets into the proper hands; those hands belonging to attorneys.

What if my beneficiary dies before I do?

Hopefully, you were their beneficiary too and are now wallowing in cash. If, however, you named a beneficiary and didn't get a return deal from them, you picked a rotten beneficiary and should be glad they are dead. You now have another opportunity to pick the right beneficiary. You may want to hold auditions for the roll and encourage the applicants to bring you expensive presents.

What is a death benefit?

A death benefit is the ultimate oxymoron. Who does your death benefit? It benefits your beneficiary who now gets your stuff and it benefits the people who make things like headstones and "In Remembrance" cards. Your death benefit does not benefit you at all because you are dead. Your only death benefit comes from the fact that once you are dead you no longer have to pay taxes or answer phone calls from telemarketers.

How big do you have to be to qualify for a group policy?

Group policies are usually reserved for companies or organizations with three or more members. If however, you are the size of three or more people yourself, you could qualify as a group. In other words, even if two people left The Three Tenors, Pavarotti could still qualify as his own group. So could Brando.

What is key man insurance?

This is a form of life insurance generally used in businesses to protect the "key man." The key man (or woman) is the person within an organization who is in charge of all the keys. They generally walk around all day with an enormous key ring strapped to their belt and is the person to call if you get locked out of a room. At night, the key man hides his key ring and if he (or she) should die, nobody could get into the building. Insurance on the key man will provide the needed funds to call a locksmith and have all of the locks changed.

Can I buy life insurance on my dog?

You can buy life insurance on any household pet including goldfish, ferrets, and hamsters, just don't expect a payoff. You can buy insurance on your pet from any matchbook advertising "$1,000 of life insurance for only a DOLLAR." The entire application is contained on the matchbook and should be mailed in with a $1 bill. When the company receives your order, they will take the $1 bill and throw the matchbook away. That's why you shouldn't expect a payoff when your pet ceases to exist. Your pet, on the other hand, will think that you are a fair and just master for insuring their life. What do they know? If you plan on insuring the life of your cat, enclose $9 because, after all, you want to make sure that all nine of their lives are covered.

What is an underwriter?

An underwriter is a cross between a fiction writer and an undertaker, hence the name underwriter. They make up stuff about when they think you are going to die. It has been said that underwriters are a boring group but there is no truth to the rumor that to liven up a party of underwriters, they invite an accountant.

What sort of questions will I be asked on the insurance application?

You will be asked questions of a non-embarrassing nature that will help the underwriters determine your insurability. Here are some typical questions:

Name: ____

Is this your real name? Y___ N___

How much money do you make? ________

Is that all? Y___ N___

How in the world do you expect to pay your premiums on that salary? ________

Are you sick now? Y___ N___

Are you too sick to pay your premium Y___ N___

Who will be your beneficiary? Husband___ Wife___ Insurance Agent___ Other___

Where should I keep my insurance policy?

Keep your policy somewhere safe yet somewhere you can easily access it. For instance, I keep mine in my sock drawer. Nobody goes into my sock drawer except me so it is safe, and I always know where it is. I used to keep it in my underwear drawer but then I didn't even want to touch it.

What's the difference between term insurance and permanent insurance?

Term insurance is available to high school and college students who have a risk of not completing their term paper on time. It falls under the heading of life insurance because if you don't get your term paper done and wind up flunking English, your dad will kill you.

Permanent insurance, on the other hand, is coverage for women who are getting their hair done. Personally, I have never understood why they call it a "permanent" when a woman has to get it done every few weeks. It is far from permanent and should correctly be called a "temporary." It qualifies as life insurance because every woman knows that beautiful hair is "to die for."

How much life insurance do I need?

As Abraham Lincoln said when asked how long a man's legs should be, "Long enough to reach the ground."

So how much insurance should I have?

You should have enough life insurance to reach the ground.

What is whole life insurance?

This is insurance that covers you for your whole life. No matter how old you get to be, whole life insurance will insure your whole life. Whole Life was originally called Entire Life insurance. Half Life insurance is also available and usually sold to clients made of uranium, which has a half-life of 235 years.

How about universal life insurance?

This plan for the 21st century will cover the policyholder no matter what universe they are in when they die. If you're in the universe of Andronicus, you are covered. If you pass away in Prioxis, you are covered. And if you stay right at home in the Milky Way, you are covered. It's universal.

What is an endowment?

This is an insurance policy for people who are very "well endowed." Dolly Parton would have an endowment policy, as would Pamela Anderson, Charo, and allegedly, John Dillenger.

My insurance agent has a lot of letters after his name. What do they mean?

The letters after a life insurance agent's name are very important and signify different degrees of additional training for which they have qualified. The more letters your agent has after his or her name, the more he or she has learned and studied. Letters to look for include CLU, CFP, CPCU, and ChFC. If you find letters after your agents name like SOB or DOA, you should probably find another agent.

Why is my insurance payment called a premium?

Your payment is called a premium because you have purchased the best insurance possible. You could have purchased regular-unleaded insurance or even diesel but premium insurance is the best way to go. Congratulations on your wise purchase.

Do I need life insurance if I am getting divorced?

Sure, why not? If, however, you are living with someone who hates your guts, don't go overboard on the insurance. The last thing you want to do is to become worth more dead than you are alive – if you get my point.

Do I need to save for my retirement?

The only reason you need to save for retirement is if you are too snooty to eat cat food the rest of your life. The government programs set up for your retirement will guarantee you enough money to buy two cans of 9 Lives per day...as long as you only shop every third day. If you want to eat real food and have access to cable TV, you had better start saving for retirement.

What's a 401 K program?

A 401 K plan is superior to a 400 K plan but not as good as a 402 K. A 401 K plan depends on the performance of the stock market for its return. In tough times, it has been referred to as a 401 KY.

Is it anything like an IRA account?

No. An IRA account can only be opened if your name is Ira. A Roth IRA can only be opened if your name is Ira Roth.

Do I need estate planning?

I don't know, do you have an estate? Do you have a big white house with about two acres of lawn and a fleet of limos waiting to shuttle you wherever you need to go? Well then, you need estate planning. If you just live in a regular house on a city street you should look into house planning, and if you live on the outskirts of town there is also trailer planning available.

Should life insurance be used as part of a gift-giving program?

Sure, if you plan on making people happy that you are dead. As long as you are alive, they will get nothing but on the day you buy the farm, they will be rolling in dough. Personally, when I die, I want people to be sad, but it's your choice.

What's the deal with those TV ads for old people that offer life insurance with the tag line, "You can't be turned down." How can they make that claim?

While it is true that the ads proclaim that you cannot be turned down but you notice that they make no mention of the fact that "you may not get any money when you croak." Old people are quite gullible which is why they wear stripes and plaids together.

I read that there are four parties to a life insurance contract. Well, I bought life insurance and I didn't get invited to any parties. What gives?

The four parties that make up an insurance contract are the insured (you); the insurance company (them); The policyholder (probably you again but it could be somebody else); and the beneficiary (somebody close to you).

You are known as the party of the first part, which means that in order for you to get invited to a party, you have to first throw a party. It's only fair. That way, you can get invited to all four parties. After you throw a party of the first part, your insurance company will throw a party of the second part to which you will be invited.

If the party is being thrown by the party of the fourth part, also known as the beneficiary, it most likely means that you are already dead because that's where they got the money to throw the party.

What is the suicide clause?

This is Santa's older brother who gets very depressed around the holidays. Fortunately he is seeing a good therapist and is on medication. He is no longer considered a suicide clause but is more like a clause who is learning to cope.

What is an Automatic Premium Loan?

If you can't make your premium payment, a man known as Vinnie Three Thumbs will automatically loan you the money at 45% interest. If you don't pay him back within a week, he will make a personal call on you.

How long will I live?

Who do I look like, a member of the Psychic Friends Network? I have no idea how long you are going to live just as I don't know how long I am going to live. My wife, though, must have some inside information because just the other day she said to me, "Would you like to know the exact date, time, and cause of your death?" I said, "Not really, why do you ask?" She replied, "Oh, never mind then."

Can you make a guess as to how long I will live?

Sure I can. Just follow this guide and add or subtract years as indicated. The final number will be your age when you die.

Start with age 72.

1. If you are a woman, add 10 years, if you are a man, deduct 3 years.
2. If you are married don't add any years but it will make your life seem a lot longer.
3. If you smoke, deduct 10 years.
4. If you drink more than a quart of gin a day, add 5 years. Heck, if you can stomach that much booze every day you are pretty much bulletproof.
5. If you drive over the speed limit, deduct 4 years.
6. If you drive on the wrong side of the road, either move to England or deduct 15 years.
7. Are you really, really fat? Deduct 6 years.
8. Do you currently have a terminal disease? If so, put this book down and go outside to smell the roses.
9. Is there anybody out there who has a reason to kill you? Deduct 9 years.
10. Does this person have access to a gun? Deduct 5 more years.

11. Are you a member of the Mafia? Deduct 20 years.

12. Do you roller blade in traffic or gargle with hydrochloric acid? Deduct 17 years.

13. Do you ramble through life totally oblivious to your surroundings? Add 15 years.

14. Do you exercise every day? Add 10 years.

15. Did you lie about the previous question? Deduct those 10 years and another 6 months for trying to pull one over on us.

16. Are you good at math? If so, you have probably already figured out that this test is completely bogus.

17. Do you chew your food before swallowing? Add 3 years.

18. Do you only drink bottled water because you think it is better for you? Deduct $5 per day from your disposable income for falling for that ruse.

19. Have you ever been "scared to death?" If so, what are you still doing alive?

Now, add up all or subtract the numbers from the starting age and you will get your age when you die. If you have already lived longer than this age, you are on what we like to call "borrowed time" and should walk gingerly.

My agent advised me to set up a trust. Can I trust him? And by the way, what is a trust?

To set up a trust, you get all of your money together in the form of investments, savings, loose change from your nightstand, more loose change you found under the sofa cushions, and anything else of value, and place it in a special account called a "trust." Nobody can get into this trust unless you let them so you really have no one to trust but yourself. If you can't trust yourself, you have issues that cannot be successfully dealt with in this book.

The person you put in charge of your trust should be someone you can trust in case you become either dead or incapacitated. This trusted person is called the "trustee" and should never be confused with a "trusty" who is a prisoner on good behavior.

By putting all of your assets in a trust your heirs can avoid probate when you die.

What is probate?

I think it's that gland in a man that gets inflamed and causes problems in later life. Either that, or it's a legal procedure to determine the validity of the will. In either case, it's a big pain in the butt.

That brings up my next question. Do I need a will?

Where there's a will there's a way so if you are looking for the way, you should probably get a will. A will is your declaration of who gets what after you cease to be. If you want to make sure that your brother-in-law Iggy gets your golf clubs, put it in the will. If you want to be sure that your kids get your collection of TV Guide magazines, put it in the will. If you want to make sure that your wife never remarries...try to get her to die before you do.

How do I get a will?

Contact your friendly neighborhood attorney and ask him to draw you a will. If he is a good artist, the will may be suitable for framing. After the attorney has made your will, he will send you an invoice for his services. No matter what you may have read in philosophy books, there is no such thing as free will.

Can I will my assets to a foundation?

Sure you can. It's your money and you can spread it around any way you desire. You can even start your own foundation, which could benefit from your funds as well as the funds of other unsuspecting patsies. My Uncle Goose tried to set up a foundation. He wanted to establish a halfway house for girls who didn't go all the way. We don't see Uncle Goose much any more. Are there any more questions?

Where is the washroom?

It's down the hall on the right. Now, if there are no more questions about life insurance, we'll proceed to the next chapter.

From Here to Annuity

It's like reverse life insurance...
ONLY DIFFERENT

From Here to Annuity

It's like reverse life insurance... ONLY DIFFERENT

What is an annuity? Boy, that's a good question. Let's break the word down into its component parts. We have **Ann**, which is a girl's name, and **Uity, which is also a girl's name**, but it is not nearly as popular as Ann. An annuity is like a reverse life insurance policy. In this one, you are betting that you will live forever and receive a payment every month. The insurance company is betting that you die before you become a financial burden to them.

I've heard about variable annuities and fixed annuities. What's the difference? A variable annuity changes over time. It changes from an insurance policy to a betting sheet for the thoroughbreds. A fixed annuity, on the other hand, has been fixed and cannot have any children.

No, really, what is the difference? Picky, picky, picky. A variable annuity is one where the insurance company invests your annuity money in "equities" a.k.a. "pick a card, any card." Sometimes you get lucky and you retire with a large annuity payout. If you are like me, however, your annuity money was invested in Enron, Martha Stewart, K-Mart, Arthur Anderson, and the Iraqi Tourism Industry. Fortunately, I still have enough money to live comfortably for the rest of my life – assuming that I die tomorrow.

A fixed annuity is just that, fixed. You know what you are getting and nothing is going to change that. The big variables in the fixed annuity department are the different options available.

For instance, you could purchase an Immediate Annuity where you give the insurance company a wad of your money and they immediately start giving it back. It's like an instant rebate. Or, you can buy a deferred annuity where you give your money to the insurance company and they start giving it back to you at a later date. It's kind of a pay now – buy later system.

The Life Annuity option is a method of payment that is known in Las Vegas as a "crapshoot." When you purchase this life annuity you will start to get payments at a specified time, and those payments will continue until you die. If you live to be 100, you will continue to receive payments.

If, however, you die the year after you purchase your annuity, your payments will stop and your heirs are what they formally call, "screwed." Your dice came up snake eyes and you crapped out. Thanks for playing. Help yourself to the complimentary breakfast buffet. This is the way to go if you really don't care for your beneficiaries.

If you like your family, however, you can purchase a Cash Refund annuity, which will take the gamble out of your payback. Like other annuities, it will pay you while you are alive, but when you die; the company will refund any money still owed to you in one lump sum. This will guarantee that they will have enough cash to throw you one heck of a funeral. If the payout is large enough they could afford full bar service and a DJ, and your memory would be toasted all night long.

Now, if there are any questions, I'd be happy to make up answers to them. Yes, sir, you in the front row.

Me?

No, the man sitting next to you.

What is tax-deferred growth?

Tax deferred growth applies to small children who are not taxed while they are still growing. Once they have achieved their full height, they are taxed like there is no tomorrow.

It's funny how, when you say the word "annuity" it sounds like "a nudie."

That was done on purpose to increase sales among older men with poor hearing.

Explain Social Security.

Why don't I just explain Einstein's theory of relativity or give you the meaning of life? No one can explain Social Security other than to say that it is analogous to a great big toilet down which you flush a large amount of your money. For a better description of Social Security, look in your encyclopedia under "Ponzi Scheme."

How do I know how large my annuity should be?

Your annuity should be large enough to pay you as much as you need each month. The real question is how much money you need to live each month. To calculate this figure, complete the following worksheet.

Household Budget Worksheet

Fill in the amount you spend for each category every month. Do not skip any category. When you are finished, add up the total amount of your expenditures and enter it on line A.

Mortgage	$
Car Payment	$
Second Car Payment	$
Parking	$
Food	$
Clothing (this figure can be trimmed by shopping at thrift centers)	$
Children	$
Pets (much cheaper than children and easier to train)	$
Cable TV	$
Insurance Premiums	$
Taxes	$
Beer	$
Lottery Tickets	$
Pay per view wrestling	$

This is Line A $________________.

If the amount you entered on line A is $100 or less, you have nothing to worry about. You are living in a refrigerator box and your stress level is under control. If the amount you entered on line A is more like $10,000 you are probably living beyond your means and had better start cutting back. If the amount you entered on line A is between $100 and $10,000, use that figure as the basis for your annuity payback.

Wow, I didn't realize I was spending that much money every month. Do you have any ideas to help me save money?

You can cut your monthly expenses in half by following these simple tactics.

1. Get a roommate(s). This will cut your housing payment by at least half. If the roommate you get is easy to fool, you might be able to save even more by having them pay 90% of the rent. If you are currently married, you already have a roommate and you don't need another one – who would, no doubt, come in the form of an in-law. Instead, tell your spouse to get a job and start pulling his or her own weight.

2. If your new roommate is also your size, you can save money on new clothes because you can borrow theirs. Again, this is not applicable if you are married unless you are one of those transvestites who like to eat, drink, and be Mary.

3. Only eat every other day. This will also cut your food bill in half. If you get hungry on one of your off days, go to the house of a neighbor, friend, or relative at dinner time and 9 out of 10 times they will invite you in for something to eat. The 10th time you will go hungry.

4. Cancel your cable or satellite TV and invest in a good quality telescope and one of those listening devices that lets you hear things 100 yards away. Then, just aim the scope at your neighbor's house, turn on the listening device and watch his cable TV for free. Of course, you have to watch the same thing he is watching. If you neighbor closes the drapes, read a book.

5. Stop paying taxes! Do you have any idea how many taxes you pay every year? You pay federal income tax; state income tax; sales tax; luxury tax; surtax; excise tax; liquor tax; gasoline tax; gift tax; flat tax; capital gains tax; hotel room tax; hidden tax; carpet tax; and thumb tax. All of these taxes take a huge bite out of your paycheck. If you were to stop paying taxes, you could save all of that money in a numbered offshore account and use it to hire a good lawyer when you get busted for tax evasion.

Those are good ideas but what can I do to earn more money at the same time?

Boy, you want everything don't you? For starters, you should probably get a better job, preferably one that does not require you to say, "Do you want fries with that?" You may want to consider a job in the insurance industry. By the time you finish this book you will know everything I know about insurance and that should be enough to get you off to a pretty good start. All you'll need then is some real knowledge about the product, a state license, and the inclination to make sales calls on total strangers.

Another way to get rich quicker is to find somebody who will agree to pay you a penny for a day's work with the understanding that each day, the rate will double. In other words, the first day you earn a penny, the second day, two cents, the third day four cents, etc.

By the end of the first week, you will have made 64¢ and on your way to financial freedom. All you have to do is stick it out for three more weeks and at the end of the month, your one-day earnings will be over $5,000,000! You can do the math yourself if you don't believe me. The only trick to this method is to find someone rich enough and dumb enough to fall for it.

The third way to make more money is to get more than one job. Since there are 24 hours in each day and you are only working for 8 of them, you still have 2/3 of the day left to make some more money. Get a second job at a restaurant. That way you will get free food too. If the restaurant doesn't provide you with food (those cheap SOBs) you can always pick up the leftovers from the customers' plates. If you already work at a restaurant, get a second job as a night watchman at a mattress factory. This will allow you to earn money and give you a comfortable place to nap.

If you need a third job to earn even more money, I would suggest something less strenuous that could be performed from a reclining position. Sell plasma. Selling a quart or two of blood each day will add up to an extra $100 a week. Plus, you get free donuts and orange juice.

Why do females pay more for an annuity than men of the same age?

They pay more because they are going to live longer. Women live from five to seven years longer than men, which means they need five to seven years more payments. This is on top of the bundle of dough they are already sitting on from the old man's life insurance policy. With this extra income, old ladies can afford to drive their cars that are so big they can't even see over the steering wheel for another five to seven years at an average speed of 13 MPH.

What is a surrender charge?

There is more to surrendering than just putting your hands up and waving a white flag. If you surrender, you are going to be charged and rightly so. Normal surrender charges include a broken sword, the keys to the royal palace, and a player to be named later.

What do the letters SPDA stand for?

SPDA is an acronym for Single Premium Deferred Annuity, which provides future payments at a future time for a single payment made now. It should not be confused with the ASPCA, which is an annuity that provides for the de-furring of your cat.

What is an annuitant?

If you purchase an annuity on your mother's sister, she becomes your annuitant. If you purchase an annuity on your mother's brother, he becomes your annituncle.

I've Seen Fire and I've Seen Theft

Homeowner's Insurance and the stuff it insures

4

I've Seen Fire and I've Seen Theft

Homeowner's insurance and the stuff it insures

If you are a homeowner, you most likely have homeowners insurance. It protects you against loss if your home catches fire, if it blows over, or if somebody steals your stuff. But do you really know what your coverage covers? Here are some of the most commonly asked questions on the subject of homeowner's insurance.

How is my homeowner's coverage determined?

First, we need to have your home "appraised" which means a total stranger called the "appraiser" walks around your house and tells you what he thinks of your decorating scheme.

Next, he checks on factors that could affect the home's susceptibility to loss. For instance, the more bathrooms you have, the more likely you are to have a plumbing problem. On the flip side, the more bathrooms you have, the more water sources you can turn on to quench a fire.

Finally, the appraiser checks for booby traps, large dogs, and electric fences which could affect how prepared you are against a robbery – or, how chronically paranoid you are.

What constitutes personal property?

Personal property is any property of a personal nature that happens to be in your personal possession during the loss. This means that for maximum protection, you should carry all of your possessions with you. That's why women have such large purses. They are protecting their personal possessions. This is also a major reason for the increased popularity of cargo pants.

What is a floater policy?

In case of a flood, this policy covers any personal property that floats. All the more reason to fill your dresser drawers with Styrofoam blocks.

Does my homeowner's policy cover my extensive art collection?

When you say "art collection" are you referring to your comic books or the pictures hanging on your refrigerator? Either way, they are probably covered. If your collection is painted entirely on black velvet or features cats with big eyes, it is not covered and deserves to go up in smoke.

What about my collection of Beanie Babies?

I can't believe you still have Beanie Babies. Haven't you been paying attention? The Beanie Baby market exploded several years ago. All you own now are a bunch of cute little stuffed creatures. If you ever get a life again, please read the life insurance section.

What is title insurance?

Title insurance is a form of property insurance that assures when you purchase a used book at a garage sale that the book matches the title. Back in the early days of garage sales, it was common practice to take an old book that nobody wanted like "1001 Insurance Laws and Regulations" and change the title on the cover to "1001 Racy Stories and Pictures" so that it would sell at a garage sale. Pretty soon, the book buyers caught on and pressed Congress for a title insurance law to make sure that when they paid for "1001 Racy Stories" they actually got "1001 Racy Stories."

What is personal liability coverage?

You have to admit that you have done some dumb stuff from time to time and one of these times it's going to catch up with you. That's why you need personal liability coverage.

You mean like the time I thought there was gold buried in my front yard and I dug a big hole and the mailman and the Jehovah's Witnesses fell in it?

Exactly. Personal liability coverage protects you in case anyone gets injured on your property, It also protects you if the roof blows off your house and crushes the

Wicked Witch of the West next door. It even covers you if you punch your neighbor in the nose for allowing his dog to roam free in your yard thus spoiling your routine of walking barefoot in the grass.

What is an umbrella policy?

This is a trick question, right? Everybody knows that this is the insurance you need if you continually find yourself getting stuck in the rain without the proper protection. Then, you have to stop into the nearest convenience store and plop down fifteen bucks for a cheesy bumbershoot with pictures of kitties on it. With umbrella insurance, you can get your money back...but you're still stuck with the kitty umbrella.

My property lies on a flood plain. What should I do when it rains?

As the old saying goes, "When it rains on a flood plain, go to Spain." Seriously, you should sell your house immediately and move to higher ground. When the rains come, you are going to be knee deep in muck and that is never any fun, although it would make a great opening act for Guns & Roses. "Ladies and gentlemen, please welcome Knee Deep In Muck."

Do you think Noah had flood insurance?

Are you kidding me? Noah cleaned up on the flood insurance he bought. Granted, he did have an inside tip on the weather forecast, but he invested every cent he had in flood insurance. He even insured stuff he didn't own. When the rains stopped and the ark pulled into dock, Noah released all of the animals that he and the family didn't eat on the trip. Noah was not a big animal lover...unless they were covered in gravy. He hated all of the maintenance that had to be done and found that he had nothing in common with the animals because they didn't even speak the same language. He was happy to be rid of them. He and Mrs. Noah quietly retired to their new mansion bought with his flood insurance proceeds. Two years later he was arraigned on charges of insurance fraud and sentenced to community service working at the zoo.

How big of a threat is residential fire?

A fire department responds to a residential call every 60 seconds in this country and they are getting very tired. Fire is a serious threat and the thought of it really burns me up. You need to be pro-active to prevent a fire in your home and that includes installing smoke detectors in the house and having a hydrant installed on your front lawn. You may also want to purchase a Dalmatian because they always seem to know where the fire trucks are.

What qualifies as a catastrophe?

A catastrophe is different from an apostrophe even though they share a weird spelling and frequently appear in crossword puzzles. A catastrophe is also known as a cataclysm, which is a small book of prayers that you study in church. Catastrophes can take various forms including hurricanes, tropical storms, wild fires, earthquakes, tornados, and presidential elections. If you encounter a catastrophe you should seek low ground, place your head between your knees, and kiss your butt goodbye.

Where do most earthquakes occur?

Earthquakes can occur just about anyplace on the planet but we only hear about the ones in California. This is because California earthquakes have their own agents that publicize their appearances. San Andreas, for instance, is repped by William Morris.

What about tornados? Where are they most likely to pop up?

Tornados are weather phenomena that are mysteriously drawn to trailer parks. I don't know why but every time a tornado appears, it destroys a trailer park. I don't know what God has against trailer parks but you won't catch me living in one, that's for sure.

How about hurricanes? What are they drawn to?

Hurricanes are tropical storms that are drawn to tourist locations. They are attracted on shore by giant Xs made out of masking tape that appear on picture windows of homes near the sea. You would think that these people would stop putting these targets on their windows but then you'd think they would move someplace safer too.

OK, OK, what about volcanoes?

The only volcanoes scientists are aware of in the United States are in Hawaii, Washington, and outside of the Mirage in Las Vegas. Stay away from these three places and you will probably be safe from volcanoes, but I'm not promising anything.

My homeowners insurance covers my house and "other structures." What is an "other structure?"

"Other structures" include anything that is not your house including your barn, garage, tree fort, bomb shelter, skateboard ramp, and those old cars on blocks in your front yard.

What is an Inflation Guard Endorsement on my homeowner's policy?

The Inflation Guard is the elite rank of troops assigned to the United States Congress to make sure that congressional salaries inflate at regular intervals.

Will my policy cover my family jewels?

Actually, your HMO or health insurance plan would be responsible for protecting the family jewels. If you were referring to the family *jewelry* however, you will need a rider on your homeowner's policy.

What kind of rider?

You definitely don't want the Winona Ryder because she will steal all of your family jewelry. You want to get a jewelry rider.

I live in an apartment. What kind of insurance can I buy?

You can buy homeowners insurance without the homeowners part. It's called renters insurance and you can't really buy it, you can only rent it. Renters insurance covers the property in your apartment including the lamp you got from your grandmother and your fraternity paddle from college. You can also purchase a Black Velvet Painting of Elvis rider with your renters insurance.

I live in a mobile home that is both my home and my vehicle. Should I buy homeowners insurance or auto insurance?

What difference does it make? You are probably going to skip town on the payments, which is why you are living in a mobile home in the first place. How do you even get your mail? What about the Publisher's Clearing House numbers? How do you get those? You may already be a winner you know.

How can I be sure that all of my stuff will be covered in case my house burns down?

To answer this question, you first have to know how much stuff you have and what kind of stuff it is. To know the answer to this, you should do a PSI or Personal Stuff Inventory. A PSI will give you a complete item-by-item inventory of your personal possessions. Then, after a fire or other catastrophe, you can match up the stuff you have left with the stuff listed on your PSI and put in a claim to your insurance company for the difference. Just make sure that your PSI is not burned up in the fire or you will be SOL. For safe-keeping, you should keep it in a coffee can wrapped in asbestos and sealed with duck tape.

If you do not currently have a PSI, here is a sample form that you can copy and adjust for your own inventory.

Personal Stuff Inventory

Name_______________________________

Address where your stuff is located

____

State (no, not the state that you live in, the state of your stuff. Is it new, used, worn, or chewed on?)

____

CLOTHING (MEN)

Of underwear without holes ____
Of underwear with holes ____
Of pairs of socks that match ____
Of lone socks with no matches ____
Of tube socks ____
T-shirts from concerts, vacations, or received as gifts____
Of these that you'd really miss if they got destroyed ____
Of trousers that can be zipped all the way up. ____

Sweat pants or other drawstring waist garments ____
Of times you have remarked how comfortable these sweat pants are. ____
Of ties that are not too hideous to wear in public. ____
Of suits that still fit ____
Of baseball caps ____

CLOTHING (WOMEN)

Even though you are always complaining that you have nothing to wear, we know darn well that there are clothes in your closet. Start by separating the normal clothes from the "fat" clothes and the work clothes from the party clothes. Make a separate list for your shoes. You will need several sheets of paper for this. List the shoes by style, color, price, and whether or not they hurt too much to ever wear again. Your compete clothing inventory should take about a year to complete and will contain over 300 pages.

FURNITURE

Living Room

Chairs (full time) ____
Chairs (occasional) ____
Chairs (portable – the kind that you haul out of the garage for picnics, wakes, and block parties) ____
Sofa(s) ____
Tables ____
Lamps ____
Televisions ____

Stereos ____
VCRs ____
DVDs ____
Remote Controls (if more than 30, fill out separate Remote Control Inventory form) ____
Boxes, Crates, Cable Spools, and anything else you currently use as furniture. Be sure to include the bookshelves you made out of bricks and construction lumber. ____

Bedrooms

Beds ____
Mattresses (with pee stains) ____
Mattresses (without pee stains) ____
Dressers ____
Undressers (people who help you undress) ____
Trapezes, trampolines, block and tackles, restraining devices. ____
Video camera ____

Dining Room

Dining table ____
Dining chairs ____
Chairs that don't match the table but are needed for Sunday dinner. ____
Usable china and silverware ____
China and silverware that has been passed down for generations and is therefore never used unless it's a special occasion like a visit from the Pope. ____

Kitchen

Pots, pans, dishes, knives, forks, spoons. ____
Appliances ____
Appliances that you never use, i.e. bread machine, yogurt maker, pasta maker, etc. ____
Contents of the junk drawer (please list) ____

COLLECTIONS

Stamps ____
Coins ____
Insects and/or Butterflies ____
Rare Art ____
Art that your kid drew and is now hanging on the refrigerator ____
Antiques ____
Books ____
Real books with more words than pictures and no centerfolds ____
Celebrity autographs ____
Celebrity DNA samples ____
Elvis Memorabilia ____
Matchbooks ____
Beer Cans ____
Precious Moments Figurines ____
Playboy Magazines ____

MISCELLANEOUS

This would include anything not covered above including,
Musical Instruments (trumpets, violins, drums, etc.) ____
Medical Instruments (scalpels, hemostats, x-ray machines, etc.) ____
Jewelry (appraised value) ____
Jewelry (greatly inflated value) ____
Christmas Ornaments ____
Sex toys ____
Semi-automatic weapons ____
Boxes down the basement or in the garage that contain stuff you haven't even looked at in years but it must be valuable or you would have thrown it out by now. ____

Now, add up all of your stuff and determine how much money it would bring at a garage sale. This figure is your net worth and isn't nearly as large as you thought it should be. You might want to go through the list again and "spruce up" some of your answers if you know what I mean.

What it all comes down to is this: If you own stuff, you need insurance. Buy some.

This Is Driving Me Crazy

The ins and outs of car insurance

This Is Driving Me Crazy

The ins and outs of car insurance

In order to fully appreciate the development of automobile insurance we must travel back to the beginning. So before we tackle anything else, let's take a look at...

The History of Automobile Insurance

"Accident is the greatest of all inventors."
– Mark Twain

"License and proof of insurance please." If a uniformed member of a law enforcement agency has just said these words to you, you could be in trouble and if you can't prove that you are insured, you are in deep spit. Well, that wouldn't have been a problem before February 1, 1898 because that is when the very first auto insurance policy was issued.

For the last 105 years you have been able to purchase insurance on your automobile but did you ever stop to think what that first policy sale must have been like? Probably not but these are the kinds of things I think about all the time. Here is what I think might have happened on February 1, 1898 when the very first auto insurance sales agent visited his very first prospect.

DATE: February 1, 1898

TIME: 6:30 PM

PLACE: The kitchen table of Caleb Johnson.

THE AGENT: Elmer "Buddy" Watkins.

Buddy: Thanks for seeing me Caleb. How's the wife?

Caleb: Oh, she's been gone for a while now.

Buddy: I'm sorry. Smallpox?

Caleb: Oh she ain't dead, she's just gone. She went back to visit her kin a month ago.

Buddy: I'm here to sell you automobile insurance for your car Caleb.

Caleb: But I ain't got no car.

Buddy: That's why I brought my brother Ernie along. He sells used cars.

The moral of the story (if there is one) is that everybody with a car needs some auto insurance. Unfortunately, when we go insurance shopping we tend to get confused by the terms. Perhaps this list will give you some clarity.

Now that you are clear on the concept of auto insurance, are there any questions?

What is "No Fault" insurance?

There is no such thing because if an accident occurs, somebody is at fault. The same holds true for a no fault divorce. If you ask either side a few questions you will soon find out who was at fault. If you have no fault auto insurance and you get in an accident, you can immediately claim "King's X – makeover take-over" and you will not be held at fault.

A different form of no fault insurance is available on homes in California. It insures against a giant fault opening up in your back yard and swallowing your house.

What is uninsured motorist coverage? Why should I pay for some monkey who doesn't have any insurance?

First of all, you should never let a monkey drive your car no matter how much insurance you have. Monkeys do not have the necessary hand-eye coordination to operate an automobile even if it is equipped with automatic transmission and cruise control. If you feel the urge to lend your car to a primate, choose a baboon, a chimpanzee, or even a gibbon before you give your keys to a monkey.

What's the deal with bodily injury liability?

Bodily injury liability insurance protects you from lawsuits ensuing from bodily injury you forced upon someone. In other words, if you punch somebody who really needed punching, your insurance company will call the punchee and tell him that if he doesn't stop threatening to sue that the same thing is going to happen to him again...with vigor.

What's the difference between collision coverage and comprehensive coverage?

Collision coverage is used when you are in a collision. The trick is that you MUST be in a collision to collect on your collision insurance. Collisions are never fun and should be avoided at all costs. If you find yourself involved in a collision, immediately blame it on the other guy. In the end, you may have to go to jail for a while but your car can be repaired thanks to your collision coverage.

Comprehensive coverage covers everything that does not involve a collision. If your car is stolen, set on fire, or swallowed whole by a sinkhole, your collision coverage will foot the bill. Sometimes people think about defrauding their comprehensive insurance by "arranging" to have their car stolen <u>and</u> set on fire. If you are guilty of this activity, don't think you got away with anything. The authorities know all about it and it is only a backup of paper work that prevents them from getting to you. You can run but you can't hide.

What can I add to my car to lower my insurance premium?

Any safety and/or security device added to your vehicle will most assuredly lower your premium. Airbags, for example, will lower a car insurance premium by 5%. If your car is old and you don't have airbags, simply use duct tape to secure a pillow or two to your steering wheel. Anti-theft alarms are also a way of lowering your premium. If your car is less likely to get stolen because of this device, it will save you money on your policy.

If you don't want to go to the trouble and expense of having your car fitted with an alarm system you can do what my cousin Elmer did. Every time he gets into the car, he puts his 100-pound Rottweiler named Günter in the backseat. He gives him plenty of food and water and things to read and Günter stays in the car all day. If anybody other than Elmer tries to open the door, Günter gets the additional treat of a human arm or hand.

What's a claim adjuster? Is it like a chiropractor?

Actually, no. A chiropractor is an adjustment claimer but a claims adjuster is completely different. When you submit a claim to your insurance company, the claims adjuster takes a look at it and adjusts the amount to what the company feels like paying you. It is usually between 30 and 50% of what you claim so a claims adjuster has to be very good at math.

What is the process for making a claim?

First, you find out if there is any gold on the land by "panning," "mining," or "asking around." Once you have determined that there is gold in them thar hills, you stake your claim by driving some stakes into the ground with the butt of your gun and repeating the words, "I hereby claim this claim in the name of

Spain." If any of your stakes are in the wrong place you should not attempt to adjust them yourself, this is what a claims adjuster is for.

How many estimates do I need on the damage done to my car?

The insurance company requests three estimates but I suggest you get close to 100. Whenever you go to a body shop to get an estimate, they usually offer you a complementary cup of coffee. If you visit 100 body shops that's 100 cups of free coffee or approximately 12.5 gallons. When you submit three estimates to the insurance company you still have 97 estimates left. You can sell these on eBay to somebody who has been in an accident and either doesn't have the time to get their own estimates or just doesn't care for free coffee.

What is the safest car to drive?

According to a recent ersatz survey of fabricated drivers, the safest car on the market today is the Humvee, affectionately known as a Hummer. They are safe because they cost so much to insure that they never leave the garage. When you see a Humvee on the street steer clear of it. The driver probably can't afford any insurance.

According to my findings, the safest car you can actually drive is the Bumper Car. We've all driven these at the amusement park and aimed for other drivers but nobody ever suffered serious injury nor was there any serious body damage done to the cars. If we all drove Bumper Cars in this country we would be much safer although we would not have any trunk space.

Another vehicle that is considered safe is the tow truck. You never see a tow truck in trouble on the side of the road. When an accident occurs, it's the tow truck that hauls the wreckage off to the dump. And you never see a tow truck run out of gas. If you want a maintenance free vehicle with a good accident record, get yourself a tow truck. *The preceding paragraph was sponsored by the United Tow Truck Dealers of America.*

If I rent a car do I need to buy their insurance?

Do you need to? My friend, buying the insurance when renting a car is the greatest deal in the world. For only $9.95 a day you will maintain ZERO responsibility over that vehicle. Drive it the wrong way down a one-way street if you like. Heck, drive it on the sidewalk if you so desire. You have full insurance. Drive through the bad part of town and collect a few bullet holes in the trunk. You have total coverage. By all means, always take the extra insurance offered by car rental agents...especially if you don't have a license.

Do you know any safe driving tips that can help me to become a better driver and therefore lower my insurance rate?

Yes I do. I call them...

Dale's Safe Driving Tips

1. Before you begin driving, take the time to adjust the mirrors, the seat, the temperature, the radio station, the headlights, and your cup holder. If you do all of this before you begin driving, it will eliminate many of the distractions you would face by making adjustments later on. Of course, if you do all of this before driving you would be a half hour late for work. You can make up the time by shaving and/or applying your makeup on the way to work.

2. Always make sure you have enough gasoline. Before you venture out, make sure that you have enough gas in case of an emergency. You never know when a devil car like that one in the Steven King book will chase you all over town. Some people call this tip "paranoia" but I always say "better safe than sorry."

3. Always wear clean underwear. Your mom has told you this all of your life but she said it because it's true. Scientific tests have shown that people wearing clean underwear are better drivers than those wearing dirty underwear. Researchers found that dirty underwear can cause itching. This will cause the driver to shift uncomfortably in his seat and will ultimately result in scratching. The scratching could cause a driver to take at least one hand off the steering wheel. Vigorous or intense scratching could cause the driver to veer off the road and into a ditch. Why take chances?

4. Don't eat while driving. This means you, Porky. Stop stuffing your pie hole while you are operating a 3,000 pound piece of equipment. If you have to eat something while you are driving,

eat something in a small convenient size, like a McNugget. Attempting to eat a foot long sub while going over the speed limit is just a bad idea.

5. Use your horn. Most of us use the horn only to express displeasure with the actions or reactions of another driver. If the light turns green and they don't move, we blow the horn. If they try to pull into the same parking space we are pulling into, we blow the horn. And if traffic has come to a complete standstill, we blow the horn along with everybody else in a strange belief that the sound will make the traffic move. From now on use your horn in a positive manner to promote safe driving. If you feel more comfortable when there are no other cars close to yours, lay on the horn until they all back away. When a pedestrian is crossing in front of your car in a crosswalk, hit the horn just as they get in front of your vehicle. They might jump a foot or two in the air but your "toot" will let them know that you see them.

6. Make your car visible to others. If people don't know you are there, they might hit you. Make your car stand out by painting it bright yellow and covering it with a variety of bumper stickers that express your personal philosophy like "Go Ahead And Honk – I'm Reloading" or "My Kid Beat Up your Honor Student." Other drivers will quickly notice your car on the road and will keep out of your way. There is a far smaller chance of your car getting hit if others can see it. Of course, there is also a greater chance that your car will get hit by other drivers who see it but either take offense to your choice of bumper stickers or just think you are a doofus driving an ugly car.

What is out of state coverage?

We all know that what "happens out of state stays out of state," but sometimes you need some extra coverage. The amount of out of state coverage you will need depends upon what state you are from and which state you will be traveling to. For instance, if your car has California plates and you are driving in Nevada, you won't need very much out of state coverage. Nevada and California get along well and there is little or no animosity between them. That means that as an out-of-stater, you will not be targeted by the hometown drivers. They won't purposely cut you off, tailgate, or give you the finger.

If, however you are driving a car with New York plates in Alabama, you will need quite a bit of out of state coverage. They don't take kindly to your kind down there and if your car has a "Senator Clinton" bumper sticker, it will be run off the road by a John Deere tractor.

Why are we supposed to pull off to the side of the road when an ambulance comes by?

Pulling off to the side of the road in this situation is a matter of common road courtesy. The ambulance is on a mission of mercy, taking somebody to the hospital who was injured in a car accident and all other vehicles on the road should give it priority. This procedure should be followed when you encounter any of these vehicles on the road:

Ambulance

Fire Truck

Police Car

Any car with a rifle barrel sticking out of the window.

Any car currently on fire.

The pizza delivery guy – Hey if that was your pizza you'd want other people to get out of the way wouldn't you?

I like to talk on my cell phone when I drive. Does my insurance cover this careless act?

Why don't you stick a burning hot cup of coffee between your legs while you're at it you moron? If there is one thing drivers do not need any more of it is distractions. It's bad enough they put that warning on the rear view mirrors that "Objects in mirror are closer than they appear." Not only do we have to worry about driving safely but now we have optical illusions in our mirrors. Put your phone away while you are driving. No matter what you think to the contrary, you are not that important and it is not a matter of life and death if you don't answer the phone right at this moment.

I have been told that I should keep my car in good working order to help prevent mishaps. What exactly do I need to do?

Every car should be kept in good running order and you can keep your auto running in top form if you follow these simple steps.

1. Change the air in the tires on a regular basis. Cars run better on fresh air.
2. Keep potpourri in the ashtray. A fresh smelling car will keep you alert and awake on long drives.
3. Lubricate cup holders every 200 miles.
4. Fill the windshield washers with colored water. It will still clean the windows but it will look much more festive.
5. Every time you start the car, make sure that nobody has messed with your radio selections. Nothing is more distracting for a driver than pressing a button that he thinks will take him to his favorite rock station and he winds up listening to a religious talk show instead.
6. Check the light bulb in the glove compartment. If it goes out on a long trip you won't be able to find the wet naps you keep there for emergencies.
7. Once a month, clean out the backseat. Remove all donut boxes, empty soft drink bottles and cans, fast food wrappers, newspapers that you picked up in the driveway on the way to work and never got around to reading, along with any junk you may have back there. This tip doesn't really make your car any safer to drive but it correlates to the clean underwear principal. If you get in an accident, you don't want the guys who tow your wreck of a car away to make fun of your messy back seat.

I have three kids and when they act up in the backseat, it can be very distracting. What can I do?

Who do you think I am, Dr. Phil? I can't tell you how to discipline your little brats other than to use the technique my dad used which was to drive with your left hand and blindly swing at them in the back seat with your right. Of course, if you are from England, you would drive with the right hand and swing with the left. If you are lucky enough to drive one of those snappy new mini vans with the VCR player for the kids, you can punish them more effectively by making them watch educational TV.

If I drink when I'm driving will I still be covered?

Yes, by a white cotton sheet. No extra charge for the toe tag.

We're All HMO Sapiens

The near truth about health insurance

We're All HMO Sapiens

The near truth about health insurance

Health insurance was invented 30 days after Hippocrates submitted his first bill. It was for 50 drachmas to cover an appendectomy and a tummy tuck. This may not seem like much but 50 drachmas in 435 BC would equate to over $127,000 today. No wonder there was such a need for insurance.

Hippocrates went on to become the most prominent physician of his time. He was also the only physician of his time so the competition for "most prominent" was not too intense. Hippocrates' two most significant contributions to the medical profession were 1. Magazines in the waiting room. 2. The unique weight loss technique he called Hippo-Suction.

Health insurance has been in effect ever since and is now a big part of all of our lives. I remember first learning about it when I was in grade school. We had to take insurance forms home to our parents in case they wanted to purchase accident insurance on their kids. On the surface this seemed like a good idea with the health and welfare of the children in mind. Then I discovered otherwise.

My parents always took the accident insurance on me and I thought they were worried that I might get hurt. One day, I looked at the policy and saw the payouts for various claims. Loss of one hand or one foot – $10,000. Loss of two hands or two feet or a hand and a foot $25,000. Loss of one eye – $50,000. I was a human lottery ticket with a big potential payday.

From that day, I have been afraid of health insurance until I realized that we are only afraid of that which frightens us. No, that's not right. We're only afraid of things we know nothing about. That's the same reason we are afraid of women.

But I was not to be stymied in my search for healthcare insurance wisdom and I searched through reams and reams of paper looking for the answers. Rather than curse the darkness, I chose to light one little candle...which is not a good thing to do when you're sitting among reams and reams of paper, unless you have the proper fire insurance.

On the following pages is everything I learned in my quest for healthcare knowledge. Now then who has a health insurance question?

My husband makes me sick. Is this covered by healthcare?

Unless you have a provable allergy to your husband, you are stuck with him and your sickness is not covered. You may wish to look at your other insurance policies however and just check to see if his life insurance policy pays double indemnity if he "accidentally" falls off of the roof.

I think I'm going to self-insure. What do you think about that?

I think self-insurance is a great idea if you are also going to self-treat whatever ails you. If you break your leg you can wrap it in duct tape and hope for the best. If you need an appendectomy, the self-treatment becomes a little more difficult. You'll need to get a very sharp knife, a needle and thread, a series of mirrors to see what you're doing, and a case or two of Jack Daniels for an anesthetic.

So you don't think self-insurance is a good idea?

It's a great idea if your dad is a doctor, your mom is a dentist, your brother is an optometrist, and your sister owns a hospital. Other than that, you had better hope you don't ever get sick.

Does my healthcare insurance cover alternative medicine?

Only if your fung shui is in alignment with the herbal acupuncturist crystal reading psychic.

My health plan calls for me to get a second opinion before beginning treatment. If I'm already sick, why do I need a second opinion?

You need a second opinion? OK, here's one...you're ugly too!

I am covered by major medical. What exactly does that mean?

Major Medical is an accomplished U.S. Army surgeon with over 40 years experience. If you got him assigned to your policy you are one lucky guy. I know a guy who had all of his medical work done by General Disaster and it wasn't pretty. Especially his breast implants.

What are scheduled benefits?

Scheduled benefits are those that are done right on schedule, sort of like the oil changes for your car. Among the scheduled benefits that are covered are periodic weigh-ins, blood pressure checks, and some rather disgusting things requiring a rubber glove.

What is the benefit of having managed care?

It's a lot better than unmanaged care. If you are sick, you want to know that somebody is in charge. This is the responsibility of the manager. If there is no manager managing your care, your healthcare will be done willy nilly and you may wind up with an enema when you really need an aspirin.

What are pre-existing conditions?

By definition, pre-existing conditions are conditions that were around before they existed. It's a philosophical conundrum like the pre-boarding announcement at the airport. How can you board the airplane before you get on?

What is an HMO and what is a PPO? I really want to KNO.

In today's world of acronyms, you need to know your HMO from your PPO or you will soon be SOL. Let's start with an HMO.

HMO stands for Handy Medical Office. HMOs are everywhere in this land to the point that you can hardly swing a congressman over your head without hitting one. An HMO is the place to go for all of your healthcare needs as long as you aren't too picky. PPO stands for Pretty Plush Office because the folks at the PPO are doing quite well.

What is a waiting period?

This is the time you spend in the doctor's office waiting to be called plus the amount of time you spend sitting in the examination room clad in a paper robe that opens in the back.

Will my dental plan cover gold teeth?

What are you, a pimp? Nobody gets gold teeth any more. The hipster urbanite is now favoring replacing those missing choppers with company logos. You can sell the naming rights to your future false teeth by calling 800-BITEME.

Will my insurance cover preventative medicine?

That's a good question because we all know that an ounce of prevention is worth a pound of cure. If you believe that marijuana will help prevent glaucoma, it would mean that an ounce of prevention...is about $200.

Am I going to need long term care?

Well, it all depends on how long you plan on living. If you think you'll be checking out in your forties, don't waste money on long-term care. But if you plan on living to a ripe old age and don't want to be set out on the curb with the weekly trash, you may need long-term care insurance.

Long term care insurance is for the time in your life when you can no longer take care of yourself and need someone to give you sponge baths.

In the past, long term care was provided by your family, but now that you're old your kids can't wait to ship you off to the nursing home so they don't have to see you as much and can spend their time vacationing in Cancun or golfing with the CEO.

What should my long term insurance cover?

It should cover everything you need to live for the rest of your feeble days. This will include (but is not limited to) the following:

Food, comfortable clothes, slippers, prescriptions, drugs not available by prescription, things and/or devices to keep you warm, Depends, cable TV, and pudding.

Why do they charge smokers more for health insurance?

Because your habit will cause you to die but before you do, you will get very, very sick. During that sick period your insurance will be expected to keep you alive. The alternative to paying a lot for medical insurance is available from Dr. Kevorkian.

What is Blue Cross?

Blue Cross is the name of the health care plan for blues musicians. To qualify, you have to have a name that includes one of the following, Muddy, Howlin', or Lemon; or you must be blind. This health plan includes all of the normal stuff plus treatment for heroin addiction.

What about Blue Shield?

Just like a windshield shields you against the wind, Blue Shield shields you against getting blue. It's the perfect plan for people with extensive anti-depressant needs.

What is Medical Comprehensive?

Just like automobile comprehensive, medical comprehensive protects you against theft of any of your valuable organs. I'm sure you heard about that guy in Las Vegas who met a woman who drugged his drink and he woke up the next morning in a bathtub full of ice with his kidneys missing. Well, if that guy had medical comprehensive he would be able to get another set of kidneys at no cost. The same holds true for John Bobbit, who, thank goodness, had medical comprehensive with a $200 deductible, but when you lose something important like he did, $200 seems like a small price to pay for its restoration.

My policy states that I am responsible for out of pocket expenses. What exactly are out of pocket expenses?

These are expenses that come directly out of your pocket, usually for things like tolls, newspapers, or pay phone calls. This is why you should never carry much money in your pockets. The less you have in there, the lower your out of pocket expenses will be.

What is Non Cancelable insurance?

This insurance cannot be canceled. It should never be confused with less known **Nun Cancelable** insurance which can be canceled at any time by Sister Mary Underwriter.

My policy is guaranteed; what does this mean?

A guarantee is good for the life of the policyholder. When you die, <u>nothing</u> is guaranteed.

My insurance policy states that it is "conditionally renewable." What does that mean?

It means that you should stay healthy. Ha, ha, got you on that one. A conditionally renewable policy means that the policy will be renewed depending upon the condition of your policy. If you keep your policy wrapped in plastic in a safe deposit box, it will be in excellent condition and available for renewal.

If you stuff your policy in the back of your kitchen junk drawer or use it to mop up spills in the garage, it is most likely in very poor condition and may not be renewed. The insurance company figures that if you don't keep your policy in good condition, you probably don't do very much for yourself either.

What is the difference between Medicare and Medicaid?

Medicaid is an annual concert fundraiser to support America's pharmaceutical companies. Similar to Farm Aid and Live Aid, Medic Aid features many of the top performers from rock and roll and country music. Additionally, they have Evil Kneivel's son Robbie who will break every bone in his body for a medical charity. Medicare, on the other hand, is a fairy tale for the elderly.

I guess the best way to keep my health insurance costs down is to stay healthy. Do you have any tips on this?

A healthy lifestyle will keep you healthy as long as you don't contract some mysterious disease for which there is no cure. Let's face it, you could be the healthiest guy in the world but if you come in contact with the germs that cause Peruvian Death Fever, you are about to buy the farm anyhow. Good health only goes so far in the real world because you never know when you will meet a viral spore with your name on it.

If you still want to attempt to stay healthy, you should start by eating right. This means plenty of vegetables, fiber, and things that taste bad but keep you regular. Then, add torturous exercise that includes running, lifting, and sweating. If you do both of these things you will live five years longer – five long, feeble, incontinent years – but that's your decision.

What are the best exercises to do?

That depends on how you are defining "best." To improve your cardio-vascular system and keep you fit, the "best" exercises would be walking or running. To improve your overall physical conditioning, you need to add exercises that involve lifting weights and getting hernias. But if your definition of "best" is the exercise that requires the smallest effort I would recommend "jumping" to conclusions, "jogging" your memory, and "pumping up" your opinion of yourself.

But if your concept of "best" is the one that combines both strength training, self esteem, and drinking into one effort then I would recommend Dale's Best Exercise©.

Start by purchasing three cases of your favorite canned beer. Lift one case over your head and press it up and down a few times. If it feels light, attach a second case to it with duct tape – which you should have in your home security preparedness kit. Repeat the exercise. If it's still too light, add a third case. One case of canned beer weighs approximately 19 pounds. Two cases weigh 38 pounds and all three cases together give you a weight of 57 pounds.

Now, lift your weight over your head and press it ten times. Good job. You deserve a beer. Take one out of your weight and repeat the exercise. This time though, your weight is 12 ounces lighter. After your set, have another beer. The exercise continually gets easier for you to perform because you are drinking the weight.

You feel good about yourself because you are exercising and you've got a pretty good buzz going. Now, hit the showers.

What about eating right? Can I still have things like milkshakes and burgers?

Well, sure you can, except now the milkshakes will be made out of soy and the burger will be made of lentils and both will taste like medicine, which means that they must be good for you. If you want to eat right all you have to do is follow one simple rule. If it tastes good, spit it out.

Should I take vitamins?

Vitamins are fine but they can become habit forming. You may start out with one-a-day but pretty soon you will be popping supplements morning, noon, and night. I had a friend who had an addiction to Flintstones Vitamins and found himself dropping five Barneys, and a handful of Freds every day.

My son came home from school with some forms to fill out for accident insurance. Is it worth it?

School accident insurance offers great payoffs if your student happens to lose one foot and one eye, or two hands and a foot, but the odds of this happening in a game of dodge ball are very slim. If your school offers classes in Well Digging or Dangerous Equipment Repair, you may want to consider accident insurance...just in case.

What is a SHMO?

A SHMO is a Social Health Care Organization and at this point in time it is only a pilot program. The goal of a SHMO is to combine the benefits of an HMO with long term care for seniors. It's a good idea in theory but with a name like SHMO, I don't see how it will ever work. Maybe they should change the name to something less likely to produce a giggle like SHNOOK.

I am very concerned about long-term care insurance. What should I look for?

When shopping for long-term care insurance you first need to decide how long you want your term to be. Many folks today are buying long-term care insurance that provides for their care until they die. This can be a long time and you want to make sure you have adequate coverage. Your long-term care can take place in a convalescent home, a nursing home, or in your own home. I would prefer to be taken care of in my own home but I'd have to miss the nightly Bingo games and the terrible food.

If I get real sick, I want to be cryogenically frozen. Will my insurance cover this?

Well, it's a small world after all. If you plan on being frozen upon your demise you had better be dressed for it to avoid any freezer burn. If you dress in layers (or die that way) you should be OK until the 22nd century. And no, your insurance won't cover this so figure out another scam.

I've heard that if I save my own blood in a blood bank, they can use it on me if I ever need it. Is this true?

A blood bank operates much like a sperm bank but it is not nearly as pleasant to make deposits. Blood banks will save your blood in a special section of their giant refrigerator and if nobody takes it before you need it, they will be happy to pump it back into you. To make a blood bank deposit, a large needle is inserted in your arm and you get to eat donuts. You don't get donuts with a sperm bank deposit but the magazines in the waiting room are better.

Do I need special insurance to protect my suntan?

For starters, suntan protection falls under the canopy of specialty insurance. The only known suntan policy was issued to George Hamilton. Your health insurance policy can help pay for the carcinomas you develop from sitting in the sun all day.

I'm a hypochondriac, what sort of insurance should I carry?

You should carry as much synthetic quasi pseudo insurance as you can afford.

Is it time for the next chapter yet?

Yes.

"I Lost Da Ability to Do Dis."

The origin of disability insurance

"I Lost Da Ability To Do Dis."

The origin of disability insurance

Disability insurance is one of the most confusing and least understood of all the insurance products. It dates back to the Revolutionary War when Minutemen got injured and were no longer able to get paid by the hour.

How does disability insurance work?

Disability insurance works when you don't work, but as soon as you can work again the disability insurance stops working…until you do.

How much disability insurance do I need?

You will need enough disability insurance to cover your basic expenses while you are unable to work. Basic needs are things like food, shelter, and clothing. Since you are disabled, you won't have to worry about expenses like greens fees or dancing shoes so you've got that going for you. Here is a sample chart from a person whom we will refer to only as my cousin Loki. Your budget will hopefully be different.

Rent or Mortgage payment. If you live with your folks enter $0.	$0
Car Payment. If you own your car or drive you mom's car, enter $0.	$0
Gasoline	Market Price
Food. Use this simple formula – (2 Burgers + 1/2 Pizza) X 30 = your monthly food budget. Accurate to within 50% of actual expenses.	$300
Clothing. You look fine. Besides, where are you going to go? You're disabled remember? You don't need any fancy party clothes to stay home.	$0
Insurance Premiums – Actually, you should have a disability clause in your policies that keeps them in force when you're disabled at no cost to you. Ask your agent for details.	$0
Rental Videos – 2 per day	$210
"Special" web sites	$500
Contributions to people like Jim Beam, Jack Daniels, and Jose Cuervo.	$500
Aspirin	$50
TOTAL	$1560

In this example, you would need $1560 per month to meet your expenses while you are disabled. Please use your own numbers when calculating your expenses. Your mileage may vary.

Do I really have to be sick to collect?

This is not like grade school when all you had to do was tell your mom that you had a stomachache and she would write a note to excuse you from school. If you are collecting disability for a broken leg, for instance, you leg had better be broken or your insurance company will send over a couple of guys to break it.

I suffer from malaise and ennui. Would this make me eligible for disability?

Yes it would, but do you really care?

How long can I stretch out my ability to not work and still get paid?

This is a good question. I have a brother in law who did this for 22 years. When they caught him they sentenced him to 10 years in prison, so in reality, he hasn't worked for 32 years.

How will I receive my payments?

They will be left in an unmarked manila envelope under an elm tree by the water fountain in the park.

What if I decide not to get disability insurance?

Nothing will happen if you never get disabled. If you do become unable to work, however, you are "sucking wind" as the kids like to say. You are up the Fecal River sans paddle. You will have to pay your own bills, and when you run out of money you will have to sell all of your stuff, and if you run out of stuff you'll have to sell your BMW.

If I have Workers' Compensation I don't need disability insurance. Isn't that right?

Yes and no. With Workers' Comp, your disability will be covered if you became disabled while on the job. If you break your leg skiing on the weekend, you will not be eligible for Workers' Comp, unless you take a lot of painkillers, wrap up your leg, and go to work on Monday. Once you are at work, unwrap your leg and take a tumble down the stairs. You are now fully covered and in an unimaginable amount of pain.

Won't Social Security cover me?

Of course it will. It's a division of the United States government, just like Congress, and we all know how well that works. I jest of course. In theory, Social Security works just fine, but in reality it works as good as the Electoral College. Any payment you receive from Social Security should be treated as "found money" and spent accordingly. If and when a Social Security check arrives, pile the family into the car and take them out to dinner. Your Social Security check should cover you at any drive-thru in town.

If I injure myself accidentally on purpose – if you know what I mean – would I be eligible for disability?

How bad is your job that you want to cause yourself injury to get out of it? If you injure yourself with self-inflicted gunshot wound you would be covered if it was accidental i.e. while cleaning your gun. But if you shot yourself on purpose, you would not be covered. A tip to the wise; if you are going to shoot yourself on purpose for insurance purposes, make it look accidental. Aim for a toe you don't really need.

What are Accidental Means?

Accidental means that something happened by accident, but Accidental Means is something different because it has capital letters. Accidental Means are the means by which your accident happened. If you do something that you know is either stupid or dangerous and has the potential to cause you bodily injury, you are not covered by Accidental Means. So, if you bungee jump from a speeding bus, you are not going to be covered when you snap a vertebra or two.

What happens if I become disabled away from home? For instance, if I became disabled on a Caribbean Island, what should I do?

Stay there and order a Mai Tai.

I've heard about an Own Occupation policy but doesn't everyone have their own occupation?

Of course everyone has their own occupation but if you have a special occupation, which is the only thing you can do, you need an Own Occupation policy. Let's say that you are Zam Fir, master of the pan flute, and you have a violent lip accident that keeps you from playing the pan flute. The pan flute is the only way you have of making a living but without an Own Occupation policy, you could be trained to do something else like stock boy or lawn care professional.

Speaking of occupations, what are the safest ones to have?

Work in the postal service is considered to be one of the safest occupations unless one of your fellow employees is disgruntled. It is far safer to work with fully gruntled people.

The ministry is considered a safe profession unless you happen to be worshipping the wrong guy. Let's face it, with so many religions out there today, not everybody is going to be right and when the big day comes you really want to be backing the winner.

Working in a uranium mine is also considered to be safe because even the drunkest driver is going to steer away from something that glows in the dark. Your life span will only be 37 but you'll never have to worry about having enough light to read in.

What is the most dangerous job to have?

Human targets have the most dangerous jobs. They are the people who work with a knife thrower. He straps them to a wheel, then spins the wheel, then puts a blindfold on, and then throws knives at the wheel. And they always use pretty women as targets. Why is this? I think they should use politicians. I'd vote for a guy who did a spin on the wheel. If he got hit with a knife I'd vote for him twice.

Fishhook inspector is another dangerous job. You wouldn't want to have this person's Band-Aid bill I'll tell you that. Fishhook inspectors are credited with starting the piercing craze in this country.

Is pregnancy considered a disability?

Pregnancy is a beautiful miracle of life. If you want to look at it as a disability you may want to take some parenting classes.

What about a lazy-ass husband?

A lazy-ass husband (whom I assume is the one who got you pregnant) is not a disability. He is a liability and can be submitted for a claim on your liability policy.

If I get disabled and I use my benefits to pay my premium, isn't it pretty much a draw?

I can't believe that you figured out our scam. If you promise not to tell anybody we will give you a discount on your premium and a Perfect Pasta Pot.

Is that the one with the holes in the lid so I can make perfect pasta every time and not have to worry about burning myself because the strainer is built right into the lid?

Yes it is, and don't forget that you can drain the pasta and then add the sauce in the same pot. If you desire, you can even eat out of the pot if you run out of clean dishes.

OK, it's a deal.

Your pot is in the mail.

My policy has a COLA adjustment. What is that?

You lucky dog. If you get disabled, your policy provides you with as many cans of Coke or Pepsi as you can drink and if you ask me, there is no better combination than pasta out of the pot and a can of Coke. Please recycle.

I'm a small business owner. Do I need a special type of disability insurance?

How small are you?

I own a small business, OK? Now, do I need a special type of insurance or not?

Take it easy Shorty. You're going to blow a gasket if you keep that up and your disability policy may or may not cover blown gaskets. If you own your own business you need to protect your business as well as yourself if you become disabled. You need to make sure that somebody is still going to be there when it's time to make the doughnuts. You need business disability insurance.

So what does that cover?

Business Overhead Expense insurance makes sure that you have enough money to pay the monthly bills to keep the business open. Things like rent, employee wages, taxes and utilities are covered. Other expenses like police payoffs, political donations, and general graft are not covered.

What if I own the company but I don't do much?

This means you are definitely in management. You need to insure the people that keep your business running. They are easy to identify because they are the people to whom you have given the keys to the business. That is why insurance on these people is called Key Man Insurance.

What is a Buy and Sell agreement?

When you have a garage sale, you are offering to SELL your junk and unsuspecting strangers will offer to BUY it. You sell, they buy. It's an agreement. If you have two people wanting to buy your item, you will need a Buy Buy Sell Agreement. If you have two items and two buyers who immediately leave after making their purchase you'll have a Buy Buy Sell Sell Bye Bye Agreement.

What is the best way to keep from being disabled on the job?

Don't work. If you don't have a job you can't get injured there. To avoid any sort of disability at home, never leave your house, avoid stairs, and always wear eye protection.

Glossary of Helpful Insurance Terms

Glossary of Helpful Insurance Terms

The glossary is possibly the most boring part of any book. A glossary is a lot like a dictionary - only smaller – and a dictionary is definitely the most boring book I ever read. The plot line is very weak, the pictures are small black & white drawings, and by the time you are halfway through the book, you pretty much know how it is going to end. (The zygote did it.)

To avoid this dreaded boredom, I decided to make this glossary different. The words will still be listed in alphabetical order, just like in the dictionary, but that's where the similarity ends. There are no pictures in my glossary, the definitions are all fictional, and, to make the reading of the glossary more enjoyable, I have liberally distributed jokes among the definitions. Hopefully, this will be the most fun you've ever had reading a glossary.

A

ADL (Activities of Daily Living) – Get up. Go to the bathroom. Make coffee. Read the newspaper. Eat breakfast. Go to the bathroom. Get dressed. Go to work. Go to lunch. Come home from work. Eat dinner. Watch TV. Go to bed. Get up at midnight. Go to the bathroom.

Actual Cash Value – Empty your pockets and place everything on the table. Count up your cash…including coins. This is your cash value. Pretty sad isn't it?

I suggest saving your money. Who knows, one day it may be valuable again.

Accumulation Period – This is the last period of the school day and a time for the students to accumulate their belongings and get ready to go home.

My daughter came home from college after her freshman year with a 4.0 grade average. Since I went to the same college, she asked me, "Dad, when you went here did you have a 4.0?" I honestly replied, "Yes I did...blood-alcohol level."

Actuary – An actuary is very possibly the most boring person you will ever meet. If you were to cross an actuary with a jumbo jet you'd get a Boring 747. Actuaries determine when you are going to die. An insurance company actuary can actually tell you how many people will die this year. A MAFIA actuary can give you their names.

Additional Living Expenses – This would include expenses that are above and beyond the normal living expenses and includes things like cable TV, subscriptions to Playboy and Field & Stream, pizza, beer, and stuff we buy from the Home Shopping Network.

Adjuster – Also known as a chiropractor. This is the person that does adjustments.

An adjuster came to a home where there had been a robbery the day before and the lady of the house told him, "When I came home, all of the dresser drawers were pulled out and everything was lying on the floor." The adjuster asked her why she hadn't reported the robbery then and she said, "At first I thought it was just my husband looking for a clean shirt."

Agent – Andy Warhol put it best when he said, "Everyone in America will be an insurance agent for fifteen minutes." If you are not now nor have ever been an insurance agent, you know at least three people who currently are.

Two guys broke into an insurance office and had amazing luck. They escaped without having to buy anything.

Aggressive Growth Fund – An aggressive growth fund grows really fast, primarily due to hydroponics and lots of light.

Airplane Insurance – This insurance is available at machines located in the airport. You can get a million dollars of insurance for five bucks and that sounds like a good deal to me.

Annuitant – A very small insect from the island of Annuit.

Annuity – It stands to reason that if something odd is called an oddity, something new should be called annuity. When buying your insurance always make sure you get the freshest policy available by asking for annuity.

Appraisal – This is a type of church service where people pray a lot.

My cousin Tinker used to pray a lot. Every day he would pray, "Dear lord, please let me win the lottery." After a while he even tried bargaining with God, promising everything from regular church attendance to abstinence if he won the lottery. But he never wins.

One day he prayed, "Lord, why, oh why can't I win the lottery?"

And God answered him, "Gimme a little help here. Buy a ticket!"

Appurtenant structures – I think this is where renters live. No, I'm sorry, those are apartment structures. Appurtenant structures are those that are very significant and essential. Whoops, wrong again. Those are important structures. To be honest with you, I have no idea what appurtenant structures are but if you have some you should probably get them insured.

A prospective renter was examining an apartment and noticed some odd stains on the wall of the kitchen. He asked the rental agent about them and was told, "The guy who lived here before was an inventor and worked a lot with explosives." The renter said, "So those stains are of stuff that went wrong?" "No" said the agent, "Those stains are the inventor."

Arbitration – If you think your team should pay you more money because you had one good year pitching or hit 50 home runs and they think you are full of crap, you have to go into arbitration where an unbiased judge will decide the outcome. If you want a fair shake you should probably tip the unbiased judge a couple thousand under the table.

Assignment – Read the first 200 pages of "War and Peace" and come to class ready to discuss the benefits of each. Also, write a 500 word sales pitch to get Tolstoy to buy annuity.

Automatic Premium Loan – Not only can we offer you a fully automatic premium with air conditioning and power seats, but we can get you an automatic premium loan to pay for it.

My new car has something that will last a lifetime. The payments.

B

Bad Faith – I think this is like devil worship.

Beneficiary – This is the person or persons to whom you are leaving the proceeds from your life insurance policy. In other words, when you die, these people get rich. They <u>owe</u> you man. If you are willing to make them rich some day they owe you big time right now. Remind your beneficiary of this whenever you see him or her. Then, ask them to paint your house. If they refuse, get yourself a new beneficiary.

A new arrival showed up in Heaven and St. Peter looked him up in the book. "Hey, you're not supposed to be here for five more years," St. Peter said, "Who the heck was your doctor?"

Benefits – There are many benefits to owning insurance. If you get sick, or injured or dead you could wind up getting money from your insurance company and any time somebody gives you money, I call it a benefit.

Binder – 1. An obligation by the insurance company to put the coverage in force before the actual policy is issued. 2. The three ring notebook that you keep your policy in. 3. Cheese.

Bodily Injury – When you injure your whole body, it is called a bodily injury. If you just hurt your head, it is called a head injury, if you just injure your hand; it's called a handy injury. By law, at least 51% of your body must be injured in order to claim it as a bodily injury.

Bonds – The home run king. Barry Bonds holds the Major League Baseball record for hitting over 6,000 home runs in 2001. At least it seemed like that many to visiting pitchers.

A baseball team was negotiating with one of its star players when stakes were getting very high. The team had offered an insurance policy worth $10 million, an annuity worth $5 million a year when he retired, and a bonus of $2 million if the player led the league in RBIs. After hours and hours of bargaining, it seemed like the deal was going to be finalized when everything came crashing down. The team president asked the general manager what had gone wrong, "We're giving this guy millions. What's the problem?" The GM replied, "He also wants $100 in cash."

Breach of Contract – There are no "take-backs" in insurance. There are also no "makeover takeovers" in insurance nor are there any "mulligans." If you try any of these little tricks, you may be sued for breach of contract and that is not a good thing.

Broker – This is how you will wind up if you make bad investments. You will be broker than you were when you started.

C

Cancellation – This definition has been stopped, withdrawn, annulled, revoked, and/or terminated until further notice.

Cap – A head covering featuring the logo of your insurance company.

> *A small boy and his grandmother were visiting the beach and walking along the shore when a big wave crashed and pulled the little boy out to sea. The grandmother screamed for help and a life guard jumped into the water. After about 20 minutes of battling massive waves, the life guard brought the little boy to shore, safe and sound. The grandmother hugged the boy and then looked up at the life guard to say, "What happened to his hat?"*

Cash Value – The value of cash. For instance, if you have a one-dollar bill in your pocket, your cash value is one dollar. If you have two tens and a five in your pocket, your cash value is twenty-five dollars. If your cash value gets down to zero, you will have to visit an ATM.

Casualty Insurance – Do you want to know why those people in the Godzilla movies look so scared? They didn't have casualty insurance. You should protect yourself now in case your town gets over run by giant prehistoric monsters that look like puppets.

Certificate – You may have not thought about giving the gift of insurance before, but why not? Your agent can provide you with a beautiful gift certificate that you can present to your loved one showing that they are insured for $1million dollars and you are the beneficiary. It's better than giving a pair of socks again this Christmas.

Claim – This is a one-eyed clam. Get it? A "c-l-a-m" with one "i"...a one-eyed clam. This is a form of humor known as a pun – a stupid pun – but a pun no less and like all puns, it should be avoided if at all possible. They're just not punny.

When they raffled off the deceased at his funeral, it was referred to as a "dead giveaway."

A boy was bagging groceries at a supermarket. One day the store installed a machine for squeezing fresh orange juice. Intrigued, the young man asked if he could be allowed to work the machine, but his request was denied. Said the store manager, "Sorry, kid, but baggers can't be juicers."

Close – 1. What you should wear to an appointment with an insurance professional. If the agent agrees to see you without close, or nekkid, they are not professionals. 2. What the insurance agent will do during the appointment at 2 to 3 minute intervals because he's really hoping for a commission.

COBRA – 1. A big scary snake. 2. A powerful muscle car. 3. The Consolidated Omnibus Budget Reconciliation Act of 1985 that requires employers to extend the health coverage of an employee for up to 18 months after they leave a job. And you didn't think you were going to learn anything useful from this book.

Coinsurance – This is insurance you can get on your valuable coin collection.

COLI – Corporate Owned Life Insurance. It is frequently confused with **E-COLI**, a nasty bacteria that will cause you to spend a lot of time in the washroom.

Collision Insurance – Collision Insurance – If you plan on hitting anybody when you are driving, you had better buy some collision insurance. This is especially true if you drive a bumper car.

> *An attorney and a doctor crashed into each other on a slippery street. Neither was hurt but both were shaken up. The attorney reached into the glove compartment of his car and pulled out a small flask of whiskey. He handed it to the other driver and said, "Here, have a swig to calm down." The doctor took a healthy gulp and handed the flask back to the attorney saying, "Why don't you have a belt too." The attorney replied, "Thanks, but I think I'll just wait until after the police have been here."*

Colonic – This is what the other guy's attorneys will make it feel like if you get into an accident that is your fault and you don't have any insurance.

Commercial Insurance – Wouldn't you like to be able to watch an entire television program with out seeing any commercials? Sure you would but that's not going to happen. You can, however, protect yourself from being exposed to commercials at the movie theater, in line at the supermarket, or when waiting in line for your luggage at the airport. All of these places have been known to air commercials and if you have commercial insurance and get exposed to one of these ads, somebody owes you money.

Commission – This is how your insurance agent gets paid. When you buy a policy, he or she gets a commission. Usually the commission is in the form of money but sometimes you get a commission like "Admiral of the Atlantic Fleet" or "Duchess of Chetchister."

Commissioner – Bud Selig is the commissioner of baseball but he has nothing to do with insurance.

Compound Interest – When you go to the hospital with a compound fracture, the doctors will look at you with renewed interest. A compound fracture is not something they see every day so they are more interested in it than they would be with a simple fracture. This increase is called compound interest.

Comprehensive Coverage – When you purchase comprehensive coverage for your car, you are buying only as much insurance as you can understand or "comprehend." If you comprehend a lot, buy a lot of comprehensive coverage but if even this paragraph confuses you, you don't comprehend much and don't need much coverage. There will be a test to determine your comprehension before any claim is paid.

Compulsory Insurance – This is insurance to protect a gymnast while they are doing their compulsory exercises, which include the balance beam, the vault, and the floor exercises.

Contingency Fee – This is a fee you pay to an attorney if things work out the way you wanted them to, but the way I want things to work out includes not paying an attorney anything so I guess this is one of those "damned if you do and damned if you don't" things. See Catch –22.

A lawyer's dog, running about unleashed, beelines for a butcher shop and steals a roast from the counter. The butcher goes to the lawyer's office and asks, "If a dog is running unleashed and steals a piece of meat from my store, do I have the right to demand payment for the meat from the dog's owner."

"Absolutely" said the lawyer.

"Then you owe me $8.50. Your dog was loose and stole a roast from me today."

The lawyer, without a word, writes the butcher a check for $8.50 (attorneys don't carry cash). Several days later, the butcher opens the mail and finds an envelope from the lawyer:

An invoice: Consultation..........$200.

Editor's note: This joke, along with a lot more, is from "The Lawyer's Joke Book – There are some things a rat just won't do." By John Patrick Dolan and Dale Irvin. You can order it in the back of this book or from www.daleirvin.com.

Concealment – This is a combination of two words, conceal and cement. When the mob wants to conceal something, they put his feet in cement and toss him in the river. He is now permanently in concealment.

Conditions – Fairly mild today with southeasterly winds and temperatures in the low 70's.

Consequential Loss – If you commit a crime and get caught, you will consequently lose your freedom and go to prison. This is a consequential loss.

Contract – If you get one of these placed on you, plan on spending a lot of time in concealment.

Conversion Rights – This is America and you have the right to convert to any religion you want to.

The town madam wanted to make a rather large donation to the local church but the church elders debated the contribu-

tion. Due to the nature of the giver, they could not decide whether to accept the offer or not. Finally one of the elders said, "Heck, let's take the money. It's ours anyway!"

Convertible Term Insurance – If you think the odds of you dying in a car accident while driving a convertible within the next few years are pretty good, then this is the policy for you.

Cost Of Living Rider – This is an addendum to your policy that annually adjusts the payout to account for the rising cost of living.

Cost Of Ryder Rider – This is an addendum to Winona Ryder's policy that annually adjusts to cover her shoplifting habit.

Co-payment – If you are going to have an operation by yourself, you're going to have to pay for it by yourself. But if you "co-operate" with another patient and have a co-operation, you will only be responsible for your portion or your "co-payment."

Covalent Bond – Unlike other bonds that are forms of investment, a covalent bond is formed by the sharing of one or more electrons, especially pairs of electrons, between atoms. It has nothing to do with insurance but now you know something about atoms that you didn't know before.

Coverage – This statistic is usually listed right on the side of the paint can. For instance, a gallon of latex semi-gloss will have a coverage of 800-1000 square feet. If you are painting over that black ceiling in the bedroom that seemed like such a good idea before you got married your coverage will be a lot less.

A rather dim witted but well-meaning workman was looking for jobs door to door. He said he could do anything in the home repairs arena. One person told him that he would give *him $50 to paint the porch in back of the house. The workman agreed and was given a gallon of gray paint. After an hour, he was knocking at the front door to tell the occupant that he was all done with the painting. As the homeowner handed him the $50 the painter said, "Just for the record sir, that ain't no porch you got in the back, that's a Mercedes."*

Credit Life Insurance – Insurance you can pay using your credit card. If you prefer to pay with a debit card you can get debit insurance. If you want to pay for your insurance in cash you are known as a preferred customer.

Current Rate – About 45 cents per kilowatt give or take an ampere is the rate for electrical current.

D

Damages – I have found that the ages between 55 and 65 are the damn ages. You walk around all day saying things like, "Damn, I can't find my glasses," "Damn, what the heck was I supposed to buy at the store," "Damn, this stupid Viagra doesn't work."

Viagra is now available in liquid form for the busy executive who likes to come home from work and pour himself a stiff one.

Death Benefit – The ultimate oxymoron. Your death does you no good whatsoever. If you were a serial killer or international terrorist, your death would benefit all of the rest of us but it still doesn't get you out of your reservation with Beelzebub.

Declarations Page – This is the first page of your insurance policy that declares things your agent didn't feel comfortable saying to you in person. A typical declarations page could contain declarations like, "You're fat. You're ugly too. Your dog is ugly. Your wife could have done much better. Your feet stink."

A man walks into a pet shop and sees a parrot right up front. He looks at the parrot and it says, "Hey buddy, hey buddy."

The man is a little startled by the parrot's conversation and says, "What?"

The parrot replies, "Your wife is ugly."

The man ignores the parrot's comments and leaves the store. He comes back the next day and sees the same parrot who summons him with the words, "Hey buddy, hey, buddy."

Once again the man replies by saying, "What?"

Once again, the parrot chimes, "Your wife is ugly."

This time the man summons the store manager and complains about the parrot's comments. The manager apologizes profusely and promises him it won't happen again. Then the manager went over to the parrot and said, "You stupid bird, if you ever tell that man his wife is ugly again, I am going to pull out all your feathers and give you to the cat. Do you understand me?" With that, the bird nodded his understanding.

The next day, the same man comes into the store and sees the same parrot who says, "Hey buddy, hey buddy."

The man looks right in the parrot's face and says, "WHAT?"

The parrot replied, "You know."

Decreasing Term – This is what we need in congress. The first time a legislator gets elected it is for 6 years. The re-election is only good for 3 years. Any ensuing run for re-election would only be good for a year. By decreasing the terms of our congresspeople we won't have to put up with Strom Thurmond again.

Deductible – The amount that you subtract, or deduct, from your actual weight when filling out an insurance application. If you weigh 300 pounds and told the agent filling out the app that you weigh 250 pounds, you have taken a fifty-pound deductible. Why don't you just go on a diet instead of lying about your weight? You'll feel better about yourself.

Depreciation – When you bought your new car you paid $20,000. The second you drove it out of the showroom, its value dropped to $10,000. By the time you got it home it was worth $5,000. If you got into an accident and totaled it the next day your insurance company would send you a check for $50. That's depreciation.

Disability Benefit – The only benefit to being disabled is that you can park close to the store in the handicapped spots, and you can get on the airplane before the rest of the passengers.

Dividend – The divisor is divided into the dividend to get the answer. That would make the dividend the thing that gets divided, or made smaller. And with dividends continuing to get smaller, it is no wonder that the stock prices are floundering.

> *A little boy doing his arithmetic homework complained to his father, "Pa, I can't find the greatest common denominator."*
>
> *His father replied, "Are they still looking for that? They couldn't find it when I was a kid either."*

E

Easement – This is a patented product that replaces common pavement. Easement® Is a rubber based product that replaces your pavement. When kids fall down and take a tumble on an Easement® driveway, they'll bounce right up with no cuts or scrapes.

Elimination Period – This is the length of time it takes you in the bathroom. Adult males have been known to stretch out their elimination period to 30 minutes or more, giving them time to read the entire sports section.

Endorsement – When you get paid a huge amount of money to wear Nike shoes, eat Burger King Whoppers, or drink Budweiser beer, this is an endorsement. In the past, endorsements have only been offered to high profile sports figures and movie stars. I think they should be offered to the rest of us Regular Joes. Personally, I would like to get an endorsement deal from Krispy Kreme. I would eat those things all day long if I got paid for it. Of course, part of the deal would have to include a health club membership and a free angioplasty.

Endowment – See "Plastic Surgery."

It's not that she was unattractive, but every time she met a man she'd heave her bosom. And every time, he'd heave it back.

Equities – From the root word *equis*, meaning *horse*, equities are those investments you make with your "horsin' around money." When you hold an equity position with a company you are a part owner of that company. Any time you visit this company's headquarters, you have a right to eat in the employee's cafeteria.

The stock market is a strange place indeed. Where else can you lose your life savings on something called "securities"?

A stockbroker called his client and said, "Proctor and Gamble split today."

The client replied, "That's a shame. They've been together so long."

Estimate – This is when people "estimate" how much money it will cost to fix your car but since an estimate is nothing more than a guess, I'd say that your guess is as good as theirs. If a mechanic estimates that it will cost $1,000 to fix your car, you estimate that it will cost $10,000. With any luck at all, the insurance company will split the difference. You can use your newfound wealth to hire a lawyer, see "Insurance Fraud."

Exclusion – "We don't want you." "You're not on our team." "We're not takin' the fat kid." "Hey Tubb-o, take a hike." These are terms of exclusion according to my therapist.

Expiration Date – This is very important, especially on jugs of milk or cartons of yogurt. If today's date is past the expiration date listed on the food package, have somebody else taste it before you do just to make sure it's still OK.

F

Face Amount – Sometimes people want extra insurance just on their face. Movie stars are notorious for this kind of coverage. The face amount is the coverage for any damage done to your face. Face coverage paid for the plastic look favored by stars like Joan Rivers and Wayne Newton.

A doctor said to his patient, "The best thing you can do is quit smoking, cut out drinking, and stop chasing women."

The patient thought for a second and said, "Doc, I don't deserve the best. What's the second best?"

Fault – In tennis, this is when your foot goes over the line when you are serving. It is also called a foot fault. If your backside goes over the line while serving, it is known as an asphalt.

Fire Insurance – If you have a job, you should have insurance to protect you if you get fired. If I had fire insurance when I sold insurance I wouldn't have gotten fired. Oh well, live and learn.

There was a man who had no life insurance but he did have fire insurance. So his wife had him cremated.

Flood Insurance – If you wake up in the morning and your bed is wet and you know you didn't do it, you probably need flood insurance. If the carpeting squishes when you walk on it, you definitely need flood insurance. Next time buy a house on a hill.

An agent was meeting with his client and just sold him a sizable fire insurance policy. He suggested that the client should also have flood insurance to which he replied, "How do you start a flood?"

Flood Pants Insurance – This insurance protects you from wearing pants that don't come all the way down to your shoes.

Funds – Funds are groups of securities that are mixed together like a fine Caesar salad. If you don't like Caesar salad, you can order a fund that is more like a chef's salad or a scoop of cottage cheese. That is the beauty of funds. Some various types of funds are as follows:

Growth Funds – These funds are designed to grow and therefore need plenty of sunshine and a lot of water.

Bond Funds – Also known as a Bundle 'O Bonds, this fund consists of nothing but bonds. I guess you could say it's bond-o-rific.

Foreign Funds – Foreign funds feature investments in foreign companies so your quarterly report may show your investment in everything from Yen to Zlotys and extensive calculations are needed to convert the figures to US$. This is the fund for you if you have a deep affinity for math.

Index Funds – These are funds whose managers select their investments by pointing at the stock pages with their **index** fingers. A great fund for the gullible.

Help Dale Retire Fund – You contributed to this fund by buying this book. Thank you very much. Now all I have to do is sell 999,999 more.

G

General Damages – General Lloyd Damages was an officer in the British army and the man credited with inventing insurance. Lloyd established the first insurance company in London and called it Lloyd's of London. I'm pretty sure on this answer but you may want to look it up just to be sure.

G.I. Bill – This is a government program that provides financial assistance for members of the service who wish to obtain a college education.

A young soldier was making his first parachute jump and listened as the sergeant explained the process. "When you jump, you count to ten and pull the rip cord. If the chute doesn't open, pull the reserve chute. When you land, a truck will be waiting to pick you up."

The soldier checked his gear and jumped at the appropriate time. He counted to ten, pulled the ripcord, and nothing happened. He pulled the reserve chute and still nothing happened. As he plummeted toward the ground he muttered, "I'll bet that stupid truck isn't there either!"

Lower G.I. Bill – This is an invoice you will receive from the hospital for performing an uncomfortable exam of your intestines.

Group – A bunch of people.

Grouper – A fish from Florida.

Groupie – A good time that was had by all.

An insurance agent told a newlywed man that since he was married now he really should have some insurance. The man replied, "No thanks, I don't think my wife will be that dangerous."

Guaranteed Renewable – This policy has a guarantee issued by the manufacturer. It is guaranteed not to scratch, not to shrink, not to chip or dent, and not to run away. You can renew this guarantee periodically. Ask your agent.

H

Hazard – A county in Kentucky where the Duke boys live with their "sister" Daisy Duke. The boys have car insurance but Daisy has quite the endowment.

HMO – This is only one letter away from being an offensive term to some people but is really just an acronym for Health Maintenance Organization. It used to be called the Standard Central Health Maintenance Organization but that acronym spelled SCHMO and people started to catch on.

A sick man sought out the most experienced doctor he could find to complain about his aches and pains. On his first visit he was informed that an office visit cost $200.

"I can't afford that." He said.

"All right," said the doctor, "since you're already here I'll only charge you $100."

"Doc, I can't afford that. I'm taking care of my aging parents."

"OK" said the doctor, "Seventy-five."

"And I have six kids too." Said the patient.

After more haggling the price was lowered to $10. The doctor looked at the man and said, "You knew I was one of the most expensive doctors in town. Why did you come to me?"

The guy said, "Where my health is concerned, money is no object."

High Yield Bonds – If you plant these bonds in the spring and keep them well watered, you should have a yield of three to four bushels per plant. Those are what I call high yield bonds.

Homeowners Policy – If you own a home and have insurance on it, your policy is known as the homeowner's policy and it makes you the homeowner's policy's owner.

Home is a place where, when you go to it, they have to take you in.

Human Life Value – Wow, this is a pretty esoteric question – what is the value of a human life? Well, I think it depends on how you look at it. If you extract all of the usable elements and substances of the human body, you wind up with a total of $2.47. This is not a very high value. But if you look at the character and soul of the person you would have to put the value of a human life at a very minimum of $15.

I

Illustration – This is like a picture except it is not the kind of picture that you get from a camera but more like the kind of picture you get from the booth at a carnival. No, that's a caricature, not an illustration. An illustration is more like a pencil drawing or possibly a charcoal sketch.

Indemnity Payments – Indemnity payments are payments that you get if you suffer a loss. Indemnity payments are nice but the real money is in double indemnity.

Inflation – This is the most crucial element of an air mattress. Without inflation, this mattress is just a hunk of plastic and you will find yourself lying on it at the bottom of the pool. With inflation, the plastic hunk becomes a colorful and buoyant recreational device.

Insurability – Insurability is your ability to be insured. Duh.

I tried to get a life insurance policy but after they gave me a physical all they would offer me was fire and theft.

Insurable Interest – You must have an interest in the person on whom you wish to purchase insurance, otherwise, you could buy insurance on anybody in the hopes that they are going to die soon. This concept was developed to keep the Mafia from buying insurance on guys they were going to whack.

Bucky's house burned down and he called his agent to place a claim. He told his rep, "I need a check for the cash value of my house right away."

His agent told him that since he has a replacement policy that they will be rebuilding the house just as it was.

"In that case," he said, "I'd like to cancel the policy on my wife."

Insurance Fraud – This is a very bad thing when people try to cheat the insurance company. They think they can make two and two equal five but if they get caught it usually equals five to ten with parole after three.

International Fund – This is usually a jar or can into which you deposit your change in the hopes of someday having enough saved to travel to Mexico.

Investment Income – This is the best kind of income to have because it doesn't require you to go to work. It's like winning the lottery with your own money.

J

Junk Bonds – Barry Bonds less successful cousin who is in the salvage and reclamation business.

L

Law Of Large Numbers – This is why the lottery works. The Law of Large Numbers states: "The more people you can convince that they have a chance of actually winning something, the more people will join them." P.T. Barnum put it more eloquently when he said, "There's a sucker born every minute."

In the hills, the father sent his youngest son to college to learn trigonometry because he was the worst shot in the family.

When he came home for vacation, the boy was quizzed by his father as to what he had learned. "Pi r squared; that's what I learned."

With that, the boy's father started to smack him with his hat. "All that money to send you to school and that's what you come home with, pi r squared? Even an idiot knows that pie are round, cornbread are square."

Liability Insurance – Depending how good your ability to lie is, you may need this insurance. Some people, like former President Clinton have a fantastic ability to lie so they don't need this kind of insurance.

Lien – Containing little or no fat.

Life Underwriter – A person who has been an underwriter for a very long time. It is most likely the only job he has ever had.

LIFO & FIFO – These are the names of my accountant's dogs. He thinks the names are very clever but I don't get it.

I knew a guy who named his dog Seiko. He was a watchdog.

Loading – This is the action verb form of the transitive "getting loaded" and used in a sentence like, "Harry isn't here right now, he's at the bar loading." The best place to do your loading is in a specific area designed for that purpose, known as the loading zone.

Long Term Care – This is such a relative term. Who is to say what is long term and what is not. If you are 95 years old, the longest term you're going to need is a year or two but insurance companies couldn't charge as much if they called it Year or Two Care. Long Term Care sounds like a much better deal. You definitely want to have long term care if you are going to prison for forty years to life because that is a very long term.

Loss – The Chicago Cubs keep trying to buy Loss Insurance but since they keep losing, nobody wants to insure them.

Client: "Hello, I'd like to insure my house. Can I do it over the phone?"

Agent: No, I'm sorry. A personal inspection will be necessary.

Client: OK, but you had better make it quick, it's on fire.

Lump Sum – This is the sum you will receive to have that ghastly looking lump removed from your nose.

M

Malpractice Insurance – If you are a doctor with a propensity to leave things like sponges or scalpels inside of your patients, you should probably stock up on as much malpractice insurance as you can buy.

Managed Care – Managed care is like managed baseball. Your care will have a manager who will dress in the same uniform as you and make you do pushups. If you don't perform well, he can trade you to another manager.

Marine Insurance – You've heard of the G.I. Bill haven't you? Well, the Army's version of health insurance is called the Lower G.I. Bill. Marines have their own insurance. It is called Marine Insurance. If you have a problem with that, take it up with a Marine.

A terrible flood occurred and devastated the town. One man was forced up onto his roof to escape the water. While he was up there, a boat came by and beckoned him to get it.

"No thanks," said the man, "I put my trust in the Lord."

As the water continued to rise, the man was forced further up the roof. After a while, another boat came by to pick him up.

"Get in" said the man in the boat.

"No thank you" said the man on the roof, "My trust is in the Lord."

The water continued to rise and the man was forced to stand on his chimney to stay dry. As he was balancing up there, another boat came by to save him.

"No thank you," he said, "My trust is in the Lord."

With that, a big gust of wind blew the man from his perch and into the water where he drowned. When he went up to meet the lord he said, "Lord, what happened? I put all of my trust in you."

The Lord looked at him and said, "Hey, I sent three boats for you."

Maturity – That time of your life when you start wearing sensible shoes and go to dinner at 4PM. It should not be confused with immaturity, which is the propensity to laugh at fart jokes.

Money Market Account – A Money Market is similar to a Food Market in that it offers you a wide variety from which to choose. At a Money Market you can shop for the best deal in Deutschmarks, Rubles, or the elusive Polish Zloty. A Money Market Account lets you shop without worrying about how you are going to pay for anything. Everything will be deducted from your account.

Morbidity Tables – Have you ever seen a detective movie where they are looking at the deceased victim in the morgue? Remember "Quincy," the show about the coroner? Well, every week on that show they had an autopsy. The table that the deceased was lying on in both instances is called a morbidity table. They are not for sale to the general public.

Mortality Tables – The mortality tables are mathematical devices learned in undertaker's school. For instance, 1 dead body plus 2 dead bodies equals 3 dead bodies.

An old man is dying and from the kitchen he smells the aroma of chocolate chip cookies baking. He asked his wife, "May I have a cookie?"

His wife looked at him and said, "Absolutely not. You know they're for the wake."

Mahogany Tables – These are found in the boardrooms of all insurance companies and usually seat 25 for a "business lunch."

Moral Hazard – This is trickier than the water hazard or the sand trap on the golf course. The moral hazard is usually a pair of scantily clad women in a golf cart urging you to help them look for their lost ball in the woods. If you go with them, you will probably lose the match but if you don't have a lot of money wagered, who cares?

Mutual Fund – If you and your neighbor have mutual acquaintances, get them to mutually contribute to a fund to buy you guys an in ground swimming pool.

Mutual Insurance Company – This is like a mutual admiration society. They want to be your insurance company and you want to buy insurance from them. It is a mutual relationship and wouldn't it be nice if we could all get along this well?

N

Needs Selling – Insurance doesn't just sell itself you know, it "needs selling." Somebody has to sit at your kitchen table and sell you this stuff. It doesn't just walk off the shelves like corn flakes or Viagra. Insurance needs selling.

Negligence – This is the reason your insurance premium is so high. Your negligence has caused undo pain and suffering to someone else and you will be forced to pay.

Negligee – This is the reason you have five kids who will cause you pain and suffering when they become teenagers. Once again, you will be forced to pay.

No-Fault Insurance – If you have no fault insurance you are not to blame. If the other guy has no fault insurance too, he is not to blame either. The real problem here is finding somebody to blame. See: Boy; whipping.

Do not confuse no fault insurance with the coverage you buy when you are installing a new driveway. The latter is called Asphalt insurance.

Non-cancelable Policy – Don't even think about trying to cancel this policy. It is NON-cancelable which means that if you cancel it, large men in dark suits will come to your home and "explain" to you why that can't be done. The only time a non-cancelable policy can be cancelled is three years after you die, and even then your signature is required.

Notice of Loss – When you walk into your house and notice that your TV set and your stereo are missing, you have a notice of loss.

O

I can't believe it but there are no glossary words beginning with O. Oh, wait, I just thought of one.

Oprah – Somebody you should call right now if you sell insurance because you know she can afford it.

P

Peril – If you live in the south, this is a smooth lustrous gem found inside of an oyster.

Permanent Insurance – Remember the "permanent record" they kept on you in school? Well, with the purchase of a little permanent insurance you can guarantee that those records will never see the light of day.

Personal Injury –This is an injury that happens to you personally. You must be injured to receive a personal injury settlement. This goes especially for those slugs that see a bus hit a light pole and then jump on the bus.

Physical Hazard – A sand trap or a pond is considered a physical hazard. The lingering thought that you should hit an old ball because you know it's going to go in the water is a mental hazard.

Plaintiff – We all have arguments or tiffs from time to time and some are big and loud while others are just plain. A plaintiff is one of the latter.

Policy – Around my house it is the policy to pray after the meal because my wife's not a very good cook. *Editor's note: In case my wife ever reads this far in the book, I am just kidding. It was a joke.*

Portfolio – A place to keep all of your insurance policies. If your agent wants to impress you, they should give you a nice leather portfolio for your policies. If they just give you an envelope or a rubber band, get a new agent.

Pre-Existing Conditions – This is a Zen concept where you carry not only your own illnesses, but the illness of all of the people you have been in past lives.

Preferred Provider Organization (PPO) – PPO is just fun to say. Go ahead, say it. PPO. PPO. It would have been even funnier if they had named it the Preferred Provider PLAN, then it would have been PPP, or P-3. What if they named it the Preferred Operational Organizational Plan? Yikes, you'd be covered by POOP.

Premium – The highest available unleaded gasoline. Premium usually has an octane rating of 92 or higher.

Principal – In the Archie comics it was Mr. Weatherby; on "Leave It To Beaver" it was Mrs. Rayburn; and on "Dobie Gillis" it was Mr. Conklin.

A mother walked into her son's room and said, "Get up, get up, it's time for you to go to school."

The son said, "But I don't want to go to school today."

"You have to go. Get up!"

"But it's terrible there. Everybody hates me and there's all the fights and yelling."

"You HAVE to go to school today."

"Why do I HAVE to go?"

"Because you're the principal!"

Probate – Have you ever wondered how the guys on those television fishing shows catch so many fish? It seems like every time they cast their line they catch a fish and I thought it was all due to tricky video editing. In fact, these guys are professional fishermen and use pro rods, pro reels, and probate.

Proof of Loss – Well, if you don't have it any more, that is a pretty sure sign that you lost it but you can't prove that because you may not have ever had it to begin with. If you can't prove that you lost it you won't get any money for it. This is known as a puzzle, wrapped around a riddle, sealed inside a 50 gallon conundrum.

Property Insurance – This is insurance on stuff that you own, otherwise known as your property. Of course, the land that your house is currently sitting on is also known as your property but that is covered under your homeowners insurance. Of course, your homeowners insurance covers some of the property that you own too but if you want to make sure that all of the property on your property is properly covered, you will need additional property insurance.

Punitive Damages – These are damages caused by listening to bad puns like this one…

I have kleptomania, but when it gets bad I take something for it. Or even worse…

Why couldn't anyone play cards on the ark?

Because Noah sat on the deck.

Punitive damages on a farm can be set as high as four or five cows, which is a lot of *moola* if you ask me.

Pure Risk – If you go to Mardi Gras and flash your zoombas for beads, you are taking a pure risk that your picture will wind up somewhere on the internet.

Q

Quote – This is the figure your agent tells you your insurance will cost. It is a firm figure so you can quote him on his quote.

R

Rate – So far I give this book an 8. It has big print, small words, and it's easy to dance to.

Renewable Term Insurance – I wish I had renewable term insurance when I was in college because I had to spend four extra terms just to graduate. If I would have had insurance on my terms and if it had been renewable, well, boy howdy that would have been nice.

Replacement Cost – This is what it costs to replace something. Boy, you really need these things spelled out don't you?

Reserves – The National Guard.

Rider – Also known as the jockey.

A horse showed up at the ballpark, walked over to the manager and said, "I'd like to try out for the team."

The manager was somewhat taken aback by the sight of a talking horse but regained his composure enough to say, "OK, let me see you catch a few balls."

The horse trotted to the out field and proceeded to catch fly ball after fly ball. The manager said, "Now let me see you pitch."

From the pitcher's mound, the horse threw strike after strike to the catcher, amazing the manager. "Not bad" he said to the horse, "Now let's see how you hit."

The horse stepped up to the plate and smacked every ball over the fence in left field. "That's amazing" said the manager, "Now let me see you run."

The horse looked at him and said, "Hey pal, if I could run I'd be at the racetrack."

Risk – A popular board game where you try to conquer the entire world. This game is not available in those countries that are really thinking of conquering the world because we don't want to give them any ideas.

S

Safe Driver Plan – This is another term for a designated driver plan. When you go out in a group, the best plan is to have the safest driver behind the wheel.

"My wife drives like lightning."

"She drives fast?"

"No, she hits trees."

Scheduled Benefits – These benefits vary but as an example, if you worked for my company you would have the following scheduled benefits:

Christmas Day – no work

New Year's Day – no work

Your birthday – You have to work but you get a cake.

My birthday – You get half a day off to go shopping for my present.

Self Insurance – First, open your own insurance company. Then sell yourself some real good insurance. When you make a claim on your insurance you can cancel yourself and keep the money.

Settlement Options – These depend upon where the settlement is. At Plymouth Rock, for instance, the Pilgrims did not have a lot of options. They built houses in a circle and tried not to die. By the time people settled in Chicago their settlement options included a variety of houses, running water, and a choice between cable TV and a satellite dish.

Special Damages – Not only did the thieves steal your car but you had a fourteen-carat diamond ring in there for your wife, Morgan Fairchild, yeah, that's the ticket. And you had a sack full of gold coins and your entire collection of Faberge eggs. Those are special damages.

Specimen Contract – Insurance companies used to collect specimens in small plastic bottles that were sent to a medical lab for analysis. Now, thanks to high technology, the contracts are printed on a special paper that allows the applicant to tinkle right on the contract to leave their specimen.

Speculative Risk – This is the risk you take when you buy lottery tickets. You are speculating that your numbers will be chosen…which they never are so you would be just as well off flushing your money down the toilet or sending it to me.

Standard Risk – Crossing the street is a standard risk. Crossing the street against the light is an above standard risk. Crossing the street against the light – during a lightning storm – while holding a steel rod over your head is not only a superior risk but is also a dumb ass thing to do.

Stock Insurance Company – This is not a custom insurance company but a stock insurance company. A stock agent will visit you and try to sell you stock insurance using stock lines like, "Take my wife, please."

> *I went to the doctor the other day and said, "It hurts when I do this." He told me, "Don't do that."*
>
> *I asked my dentist what to do about yellow teeth, he told me to wear a brown shirt.*
>
> *My doctor told me to have only one drink a day. This one is for February 15, 2015.*
>
> *Thank you very much. I'll be here all week. Try the veal. And don't forget to tip your waitress.*

Surety Bond – This term goes back to the days of the Old West when people used phrases like "Durn Tootin'" and "Land O' Goshen." If someone asked if the bond they were about to purchase was any good, they would be told "It Surety Is!" Was this something they said just to make the sale? You're durn tootin' it is.

Surrender Charge – When one party surrenders to another, there is a price to be paid. You've heard the phrase, "To the victor belongs the spoils," well where do you think that phrase originated? With the surrender charge. You should really spend a little more time studying history.

T

Tax Deferral – This is a tax levied on wild or "feral" animals like cats, dogs, and Senator Hillary Clinton. How deferral tax is collected has never been determined but if you are a wild animal consider yourself forewarned.

> *The owner of a small restaurant was called before the IRS because of certain deductions. The auditor wanted an explanation for how the man justified deducting trips to Paris, Rome, Portugal, and Bermuda. "How in the world can you justify this?" the auditor asked, "You only own a small restaurant."*
>
> *The restaurant owner said, "We deliver."*

Term Insurance – In this great country we will never get stuck with a goofball president for more than two terms. After that America's term insurance kicks in and we get a new goofball president.

Tern Insurance – This is insurance available for various sea birds of the genus Sterna, related to and resembling gulls but characteristically smaller and having forked tails. You are probably more concerned about term insurance.

Third Party Coverage – Normal homeowners insurance will cover the damage caused to your property by rowdy guests at a party. Broken glass, structural damage, fire and smoke damage, flushing a cat down the toilet, are all items which should be covered BUT, your insurance will cover this damage for no more than TWO parties a year. If you plan on entertaining more than that, you would be wise to invest in third party insurance.

Tort – A wrongdoing not involving breach of contract, for which a civil suit can be brought.

Torte – A delightful dessert made of lots of eggs that can cause your cholesterol to soar off the chart. If you eat a lot of tortes, buy a lot of insurance. If you find that your over consumption of tortes caused you to become fat, you could sue the torte company under tort law.

Tortellini – Little teeny tiny tortes, which should cause you no health problems.

Trust – It is very important that this exists between you and your insurance professional. If you can't trust the person who is helping you plan your financial future, who can you trust? Sometimes people like Martha Stewart have too much trust in their investment counselors and that isn't good either.

Some people just trust too much. One guy told his friend, "My wife must be an unbelievably good cook. I came home early yesterday afternoon and I found a two hundred pound truck driver eating there."

U

Underwriter – The underwriter is the first person to review your insurance policy. The undertaker is the last.

The undertaker told the widow, "I took extra care with your husband because he was a fine, upstanding, caring, sensitive and loving person."

The widow looked at him and said, "We better open the casket and take a look. I think you've got the wrong guy."

Unemployment Insurance – When you lose your job, you can collect benefits from the unemployment insurance your employer buys. The key to unemployment insurance is to collect it for as long as possible. Frederick Sloogum of Pennsylvania holds the record for collecting unemployment insurance for 53 years, the last twenty of which, he was dead.

Universal Life – I think this is the name of the church that the Moonies go to.

V

Variable Life Insurance – You know how some days you feel like a million bucks and other days you feel like a plugged nickel? Well, just as your mood varies, so does your variable insurance. It is in your best interest to die on a day that you feel like a million bucks.

W

Waiting Period – Three days for the purchase of handguns. Why, do you want to know?

> *A first time hunter came back to the lodge all excited and said, "I just shot an elk."*
>
> *One of the other hunters asked him, "How do you know it was an elk?"*
>
> *"I looked at his membership card."*

Waiver – When there is an accident or a fire that is covered by your local television station, people will appear out of nowhere and stand behind the reporter and wave. That's all they do, wave. Sometimes they jump up and down but most of the time they just wave. These are waivers.

Whole Life Insurance – Once you buy it, you own it for your whole life, sort of like a bottle of Worcestershire sauce.

Will – Short for William.

Workers Compensation – In addition to his or her salary, a worker's compensation also includes vacation days, sick days, and rubber bands or paperclips taken home from the office. Try to get a compensation package that also includes free lunch in the company cafeteria. If you bring enough plastic zip-lock bags, you can usually take home enough stuff for dinner too.

XYZ

X-Ray, Yugoslavia, Zipper – None of these words have anything to do with insurance but I didn't want to leave out the last three letters of the alphabet.

9

The Close

"Just sign on the line and I'll be on my way."

The Close

"Just sign on the line and I'll be on my way."

The close is when an insurance agent asks you for your business. Unlike automobile salesmen, your insurance agent does not have to "run the deal past his manager" before finalizing the deal. In the case of this book, however, the close means that you can close the book because you are finished reading it.

I do remember a few things from my days selling life insurance (all 197 of them) and that is to always ask for the order. So, if you like this book and would like to read other books that I wrote, you can order them directly from www.daleirvin.com. Or you can talk to a live person by calling 800-951-7321.

For your convenience, here's a full list of the products I offer. Thank you for reading this book and always remember, you can never have too much insurance.

Laughter Doesn't Hurt – Hilarious book based on Dale's popular live show of the same name. $12.95

Dale Irvin Rewrites History – A very funny look at history based on real people, actual events, and totally made up stories. $12.95

The Lawyers Joke Book "There Are Some Things A Rat Just Won't Do." $9.95

Outlaws of Success – Five successful "outlaws" share their secrets of success. $12.95

Outlaw Wisdom – Book of quotes by The Outlaws Of Success. $9.95

The Everything Toast Book – Toasts for every conceivable occasion. $12.95

The Everything Barbecue Cookbook – Possibly the funniest cookbook you have ever read. $14.95

Dale Irvin Shoots Back – (audio tape) Dale has fun with telemarketers when they call. $10.00

About the Author

Dale Irvin is a professional speaker and a member of the CPAE Speaker Hall Of Fame. His speaking style is quite unique in that he is a professional summarizer. Dale attends meetings and conventions and throughout the day recaps the events that have just occurred in a humorous monologue. He has recapped meetings for the Million Dollar Round Table, The Top Of The Table, Allstate Insurance, MONY, Thrivent Financial For Lutherans, Penn Mutual, Nationwide, and many many more.

For more information please visit www.daleirvin.com.